AF471175

THE BLUE BAYS OF CORNWALL

The Blue Bays
of Cornwall

NIGEL TANGYE

WILLIAM KIMBER · LONDON

First published in 1986 by
WILLIAM KIMBER & CO. LIMITED
100 Jermyn Street, London SW1Y 6EE

ISBN 0-7183-0595-7

Photoset in North Wales by
Derek Doyle & Associates Mold, Clwyd
and printed in Great Britain by
Biddles Limited, Guildford and King's Lynn

Contents

*A map of the bays of Cornwall
appears on pages 48-9*

Acknowledgements

I offer grateful thanks to all those who have helped me in the preparation of this book. Particularly do I thank Miss Angela Broome, Assistant Librarian of the Royal Institution of Cornwall, Truro, and its Curator Mr H.L. Douch who is never far from researchers in offering them the fruits of his scholarship.

I am grateful to Colin Edwards of the County Record Office for bringing my attention to the Rashleigh Manuscript. To Kate Dinn I am grateful for her initiative in creating, on behalf of the Falmouth Art Gallery, the exhibition covering the tragic voyage of the *Mignonette*; and, too, I offer thanks to David Sharpe and Newquay Old Cornwall Society for their co-operation.

I am indebted to Edward Yescombe for my being able to bring your attention to his forbear's life as a Post Office Packet Captain: and to Charles Tarry and Donald Rawe, of the Lodenek Press, for enabling me to have an authentic view of Padstow and the Doom Bar.

To Mr Julian Williams and Mr J. Trudgeon I extend my thanks for enabling me to include an extract from an episode at Port Luney, and to the Cambridge University Press for permission to quote from *Memories and Opinions* by 'Q'.

My most sincere thanks go also to Rodger Penhallurick, Assistant Curator of the Royal Institution of Cornwall, for his very delightful map.

N.T.

Preface

As soon as the present becomes the past a new dimension is added to it: how we live and what we experience become the framework of history tomorrow. Insecure as we are now, faced with a threatening future, we seek to find consolation, even hope, from the past. The growth of public interest in the search and discovery of family trees reflects this tendency. Great satisfaction is felt when a family can trace its roots back, the further the better, from our threatened environment.

We have become disillusioned by the role played in the past by the posturings of Party leaders, pundits and Parliaments: the spotlight is turned elsewhere, onto social history, onto the lifestyle of ordinary people, onto ecology.

Here then, I seek to offer the reader a modest view of a subject rarely aired, that of the part our Cornish bays have played in our history, be it maritime, commercial, or social.

According to the Oxford Dictionary, a bay is no more than an 'indentation made by the sea into the land.' Well, when I am standing on the clifftop, on a fine summer's day, and looking out across my local bay, that of Newquay, I see much more than that. Calm, and blue, and serene it may be now, but I have no difficulty in giving equal emphasis in my thoughts to visualising its other face, one of fury, of sombre colours, of hostile motion in a panorama of greys and blacks, of white fretting and foaming and charging seas, with sparkling lines of waves leaving behind them a roughened carpet of foam. Yes, I see it all. To the Oxford Dictionary's definition of a bay I would add ... 'and alive with the waters of the sea'.

A bay, like a cat, is aloof, keeping itself to itself, living its own life in accordance with nature's purpose. A bay is a valuable food store stocked for the benefit of the community and for people far, far afield: for three centuries Cornish vessels delivered fish as far away as Italy.

A bay plays its part for a mariner, easing the way of a vessel from harbour to open sea, and welcoming the incoming vessel from far away with promise of shelter and relaxation for captain and crew.

A bay is the creator of the scene that provides me with the story of those who sailed over it or lived close by, within the sphere of its silent influence. Our contacts will vary from seaman to slate miner, from smuggler to vicar, from landowner to the last convicted white cannibal.

So come, now – join with me on the way to meet them!

This Cornwall – An Introduction

Cornwall is one of the most remarkable of the English counties, not only from its geographical position and mineral productions, but because it possesses features peculiarly its own, having little in common with the other territorial divisions of England, unless it be a part of Devonshire.

Beaches, deeply indented, lashed by ever restless seas, secluded coves with extensive sands, precipitous headlands, beautiful and fertile valleys, sterile hills with granite peaks, extended wastes, and districts boasting a fertility surpassed nowhere in our island, scenery of the grandest description, as well as of the softest character – these are all distinguishing traits of the Cornish promontory. To the foregoing may be added a mild and genial climate, a friendly and hospitable people, a remarkable geological structure, mining resources which have been unequalled in the world, the flora of a southern climate, inexhaustible wealth in its own giant storehouse – the ocean; and, too, antiquities belonging to the earlier history of the British people, and remnants of a language abounding in words derived from an eastern source, evidence of a remote intercourse with some of the most celebrated nations that now exist but in history. Such are, in brief, some of the causes that enhance the interest attaching to the southernmost land of England.

The undulations of surface, and irregularities caused by the numerous headlands afford every variety of aspect. On the northern coast the shores, which go bluffly into the ocean. When they don't dip down like that they are bordered at low water with a narrow strip of sand. Vast drifts of sand are forced up by the fury of the Atlantic storms upon some parts of the north-western coast. This accounts for there being only two good harbours along the whole length of that coast, and even those are impossible of access only too often because of the fury of the sea.

Turning from the coast to the inland of the county, or Duchy as it should always be called, the surface is remarkably varied. The highest hill is 1,400 feet, and yet there is no county in England where there is so little level ground. Along the centre there is a ridge of hills, disconnected from those at nearby Dartmoor by the deep valley through which the river Tamar winds its serpentine course nearly from sea to sea.

Cornwall is the land of the wild, the picturesque and the imaginative. The air is soft and pure; there is the voluptuousness of the 'sweet south' in the atmosphere at times, tempered by Atlantic breezes; the heaths are various, and rich to a degree seen nowhere other than in England.

So seemingly contemporary are the foregoing remarks that my reader could be forgiven for thinking they were written yesterday. They were, in fact, written one hundred and fifty years ago by Cyrus Redding. He goes on to tell us something of the people, and records his view that 'the women of Cornwall were handsome, but not particularly fresh coloured; they were modest, open and unaffected in manners, free from that constraint which was the mark of a want of good breeding, even where intercourse with society was by no means of an extensive character; making correct, as related to the Cornish fair, the remark of Queen Elizabeth respecting the gentlemen of the county, that "the Cornish gentlemen are all born courtiers with a becoming confidence". The men were strongly made, and more active than those of the midland counties of England.' This was reflected in the Militia of whom it was remarked that they stood on more ground than any other regiment of the same number. They were uncommonly well-set; their old habits of hurling and wrestling, as well as labour out of doors, no doubt contributing to their muscular power.

Wrestling was a favourite sport, but in Cornwall the wrestler was never permitted to kick the shins of the antagonist; everything depended on sheer strength. The men, at that time, were generally of middle stature and lived to be old when not employed in the mines; or, if they were there, they did not add intemperance to the confined nature of their labour. Borlase mentions a woman in Gwithian parish dying, in 1676, at 164 years old. At the Lizard Point, the most exposed part of Cornwall, the Reverend Mr Cole, minister of Landewednack, died at 120, and the sexton was above 100 years when he died. Dr Borlase went, in 1752, to see a man at the Lizard 105 years old, of a florid countenance. He stood near his door 'leaning on his staff, saying he was weary of life, and advised us "never to wish to live to an old age": he died in 1754.'

Doctor Borlase is the distinguished antiquary who was born in 1695, near Penzance. He was educated at Penzance and Exeter College, Oxford. In 1722 he was appointed to the living of Ludgvan, near Hayle, and he held this for 52 years, during which time his works on archaeology were produced, works which, today, remain primary sources of great value.

In 1752, his *Natural History of Cornwall* was published, a work from which we are going to draw in a few moments. In 1750 he was made a Fellow of the Royal Society, and given an LLD shortly after the publication of his *Cornish Antiquities*. His *Observations on the Isles of Scilly* received praise from Dr Johnson. His scientific mind ventured into anything and everything, and I find very interesting indeed one of his studies on ecology, namely the poisoning of the atmosphere by the mining industry – yes, air pollution is by no means a new thing to cope with!

As there are so many mines in Cornwall, and most of them yield sulphur, vitriol, and mundic, they cannot but affect the air with their steams in proportion to the quantity yielded by the mine, and the facility with which their parts separate and ascend into the Atmosphere. These mineral vapours ascend so copiously out of some of our lodes, or veins of metal, and consist of such inflammable parts as to take fire, and appear in flame over the lodes from which they rise, and it is a common opinion among tinners, especially those of more than common speculation, that where little flames of light are seen in the night time, there a prosperous lode lies underneath, but, indeed, the lights which are much oftener imagined, and have nothing to inform us of, but that being deserted by the sun that raised them.

On the 20 December, 1752, at about eight in the morning [the sky] became suddenly overcast, with dark red, angry clouds, the wind being very boisterous. At intervals there was blue sky, then large clouds gathered with cold showers. By a quarter before twelve, there was neither rain nor wind, but sunshine: some flying thin clouds were observed to join, and one of the most shocking peals of thunder ensued. The lightning fell with the greatest violence upon a hill in the parish of Madron where it pierced banks like a dart, furrowed the ground as if it had been a plough-share, cut off flat turves, burst rocks, split them into shivers, fell on some particular spots of rocks and splintered them as if they were musket balls. It rooted up some stones, and made its way clear under others, showing the traces on each side. The whole workings of this lightning on this hill (than which there is no higher betwixt the North and South Sea), were in length about a furlong from East to West [one-third mile]: and there was smoke seen in part of this hill as if several muskets had been discharged. At the thunder, the sheep dispersed and ran to and fro as if pursued by a pack of dogs. At Trythal, a village without tree or hill near it, this clap of thunder was so violent that nothing was remembered to be equal to it.

The experience of this storm was terrifying for the villagers. One of the most successful and respected farmers of the neighbourhood, one Thomas Olivey, had returned home for lunch where all the family were gathered. They were all in the kitchen, excepting his daughter, who was in the hall. Over the kitchen stove there was a brass pan nearly full of boiling water. Mr Olivey was sitting by the fire, his wife on a bench in front of it; and their only son, aged twenty-three was standing at the window. His father was alarmed when he found the lightning become so powerful that the back door, facing north, began shaking violently. He called to his son telling him not to stand at the window in case the lightning hurt his eyes. The son responded, and he withdrew from the room backwards, into the corner, and sat down, as he thought in a place of greater security. To this the apprentice boy gave way to laughter, which was firmly quelled by the head of the family who, luckily for the boy, sent him out of the room. Almost immediately after this, lightning struck the stack of the kitchen chimney, which was about four-foot square and as much in height. It was of hewn stone, even so the lightning carried it clear off from the house, throwing it into a pool of water twenty feet away.

The farmer himself saw no lightning, nor heard any thunder, being struck senseless with the first flash, and being thrown into the middle of the kitchen, where he remained senseless for a quarter of an hour. As soon as he came round he demanded who struck him. Mrs Olivey found herself lying on the hearth, with both her shoes, though buckled on as usual, torn from her feet; her feet were not hurt but could not be moved. Her sister was near the back door and was struck senseless, and thrown twelve feet against the heavy settle. Her son had seated himself according to his father's directions. His coat and waistcoats (for he had two on) were torn into shreds, so that it was difficult to distinguish where the pieces had formerly joined. His shirt had a rent two feet long down the back, and was singed; His left shoe was torn from his foot, and the little toe of that foot so nearly cut off that it hung by a bit of skin.

He was quite dead, though there was no sign of his being struck; nor was there any sign that the dog, lying at his master's feet, was dead, too.

The daughter received the shock in the hall; she was struck senseless but revived soon, trembling all over, her feet tickling, partly benumbed and stiff, as if sleeping. Realising the room where she was was full of smoke, and hearing her mother cry, she hurried into the kitchen, which was also full of smoke smelling like brimstone.

All this happened in an instant, an instant when all was fire, yet a fire that stopped with the flash.

Borlase writes in some detail of another occasion when lightning struck with similar effect, after which he wants to be fair to Cornwall and informs us that

> having mentioned the excesses to which the air of this County is subject, I cannot but observe that, notwithstanding this, the air is very healthy. Though we have frequent rains the air is by no means thereby rendered less fit for respiration: it is not charged with sluggish exhalations of bogs, marshes or stagnating pools among thick woods; nor do many flat calms happen, and when they do, they seldom continue for more than a space of a day: for either the sea breezes interpose, or numerous bays – and this interests us – and promontories, by opposing and collecting every current of air, promote a constant flow of wind one way or other round their extremities, so that mists seldom rest long. Nor can the saltness of the air, nor the mineral exhalations be said to make the air sickly, as many instances of long life being found here as in any other part of England, so happily do these seeming extremes correct and qualify one another, and by mixture and proportion, rectify and keep the air in a wholesome temperature.

Let us recall that this judgement on the air pollution situation falls on our ears from a voice in the middle of the eighteenth century, and our reaction as we read it is as lively as it was for those contemporary readers who may seem to us so far away. They are not. They are just a thought away.

I

Cawsand Bay

The last time I had been to the fishing village of Cawsand was after I had sailed down from Falmouth in my ketch, *Spray of Glendorgal*, to join in the welcome to Sir Francis Chichester on the completion of his first solo circumnavigation of the world. Later that day I dropped anchor in Cawsand Bay.

The scene was idyllic. The old houses seemingly coming down the slope and stopping just before reaching the water's edge. Other yachts at anchor dotted about the bay on this sunny, summer afternoon; there appeared to be no sign of anyone in the village. All was peace. All was contentment. I thought to myself, 'How could it be anything else? Even though a great arsenal housing much of the British Navy's requirements was harboured in the dockyard the other side of the Sound?' Well, I was naive, I was very wrong. Let's see how wrong.

It was in the deep blue water of Cawsand Bay that ships of our fleet would assemble for the replenishing of stores before going to sea. This was before the breakwater was built. It was to Cawsand that they would return to take on board equipment and provisions and water in readiness for further duties. For some two centuries (prior to mid-nineteenth) Cawsand was closely bound up with the Navy and its existence might have seemed to have been dependent on the Navy.

There was another phase of Cawsand life which, though long forgotten, once played a very important part in the economy of its inhabitants and the character of the bay. This was smuggling; the bringing in from the Brittany coast hidden cargoes of brandy and tea free of import tax by dodging the Customs.

At what period the men of Cawsand took to illicit trading cannot be affirmed with any certainty; but to them, when the final history of smuggling comes to be written, the doubtful place of honour will be reckoned to be theirs.

The golden age for Cawsand was the beginning of the nineteenth century, even later, for I have seen recorded the memory of an old smuggler at the end of the century who cherished his recollection of the 'good old days' when money was 'that plentiful' in Cawsand that 'if one woman went to borrow of another the friend in need would measure out golden guineas by the basinful.'

'When I was stationed at Cawsand, long ago,' said one of these old cronies, an old Coastguard pensioner, 'well I remember an old fellow, almost bent double with age, who often came down to the beach to hunt about for guineas. You see, guineas were so plentiful in old times that I've heard it said chaps used to play pitch-and-toss with them just as the youngsters do now with h'apence.'

One might ask, whence arose this traditional story. Possibly it was the reckless way in which the smugglers in the halcyon days of the 'trade' were wont to squander their ill-gotten gains, for the profits from a successful trip for tubs of brandy were often enormous.

Not until we come to the beginning of the nineteenth century do we have any firm facts, any official records of the 'trade' to build on, and on which we can rely. Everything before this is mere tradition and does not concern us here.

When the long war with France came to an end [1815] and the fighting services of the Crown were reduced, a number of privateer men and other characters which a long war invariably brings to the surface – men whose vocation was fighting and who preferred a life of excitement and danger to the more prosaic paths of honest industry – these were let loose upon the country. And these men, for want of more exciting occupation, naturally drifted into the ranks of smugglers, with the result that in a short time of the return of peace there was a great resurgence of smuggling all along the coasts of the United Kingdom.

The termination of the war, however, also enabled the Government to devote more attention than had been possible, hitherto, to the frightful leakage that had been going on for years past in the revenue in consequence of the activities of the smugglers; and as the service of a large number of soldiers and sailors who had been fighting their country's battles were now available there was at once organised, for the first time in the nation's history, a really efficient Preventive [Customs] Service. The new force was established along the south coast of England in 1816/17, and it is from the official records of the force that it is possible to compile a consecutive history of smuggling.

Of the causes which contributed to the pre-eminence of Cawsand in smuggling annals, not the least important was its proximity to Plymouth and other populous places in which there was a ready market for the sale of French brandy and odds and ends it pleased the smugglers to bring over; the inhabitants showed a decided preference for cheap spirits. With such facilities for disposing of their wares, the men of Cawsand would have been less than human had they neglected to take advantage of them; while the high duties which were imposed at this time on nearly all imports, but especially on tea, spirits and tobacco, with resultant enormous profits that accrued to the successful smuggler, gave an additional stimulus to the trade all along the coast.

But what chiefly had enabled the Cawsand men to take the lead was their possession of a class of boat which exactly suited the requirements of the trade. It was a large craft, cutter or lugger rigged, of a hundred tons and more, which had been employed during the war and carried guns not always for fighting the French only. These vessels were no longer available. An armed craft for smuggling was a pirate, pure and simple and could never be tolerated in peacetime. Moreover most of these vessels, even if not worn out and consigned to the ship-knacker's yard, were far too large for the circumstances the trade now met with. A much smaller class of vessel was required as being less liable for detection and handier in every way for the 'running' of illicit goods on a guarded coast.

It so happened that the Cawsand Bay fishing boats exactly met these new requirements. They were half-decked and were excellent sea boats and of remarkably good sailing quality; and so they came into immediate demand.

For an industry such as smuggling, where high profits tempted men to take great risks, every sort of craft was requisitioned. There were men always to be found who were both willing and eager to risk the hundred-mile crossing in an open boat to Brittany. The real 'trader' aimed at cargoes of a hundred tubs and more [each tub, 4 gallons], and these were rarely in use anywhere else along the coast other than Cawsand; and so were always in demand by traders from all over the County.

It might be thought that the proximity of a great naval port, with men-of-war constantly passing in and out of the Sound, and a staff of Customs Officers and several men in their very midst, with their cutter or cutters at anchor in the bay would be too much of a risk, but these obstructions gave additional zest to smuggling; and for many years the business went on as merrily as ever. A part explanation of this was that the public was in sympathy with the smuggler and against the Revenue man; and their attitude to the smuggler was one of admiration for an audacious man, rather in the same way that today we admire men of the SAS.

Cawsand having thus become the headquarters of smuggling in the West there was witnessed there during the next twenty years a remarkable display of enterprise and daring on the part of the men who conducted the trade. The reputation for the skill, energy and knowledge of their 'craft' which the Cawsand men enjoyed far and wide, brought about a constant demand for their boats, and, while profits remained high, there were never wanting men to risk the crossing.

With the coming of the newly formed Coastguards it became evident to the experienced smugglers that the free and easy methods of old were no longer applicable. With watchmen placed at the blue head of every creek and headland it was impossible to effect a direct landing now, even at night, while the strength, discipline and fighting equipment of the new force disinclined all but the most fire-eating of smugglers from risking a conflict. The danger, moreover, of approaching a rock-bound coast in the dark was one the owners of boats never cared to face. Hence there came into vogue at this time the practice of sinking cargoes, and, afterwards 'working' them – that was, picking up the goods from the seabed and landing them as opportunity offered, to avoid suspicion.

Now, for the purpose of 'working' the goods the Cawsand smugglers employed a six or eight-oar galley of light framework and good speed. These were built ostensibly for working the seine nets for pilchard fishing. These galleys subsequently played a very important part in the economy of Cawsand smugglers.

Having regard to the peculiar nature of their function, these galleys attracted a great deal of attention from the Preventive men, while a prolonged absence of one of them was sure to cause a flutter in the Coastguard dovecot. A General Order of the period contains the following significant remark. 'A Rocket and blue light will be fired from the Rame head when the Galleys go afloat, as a signal to Polperro.'

The activities of the smugglers were by no means confined to their own neighbourhood. They often wandered round into the North Channel [Bristol Channel] and 'ran cargoes to Padstow', but the role of the galleys was necessarily more circumscribed, being practically confined to the coast between Plymouth Sound and Polperro and the Mewstone.

They also worked Looe Island, but the happy hunting ground *par excellence* was in Whitsand Bay along the shore of which the cargoes were usually sunk. At a later period smugglers were driven further afield, to the Eddystone Lighthouse around which huge quantities of cargoes were sunk.

The display of so much enterprise and activity in the cause of 'free trade' on the one hand, and the keenness of the Preventive men in pursuit of prize money on the other, led to some interesting situations from whence arose many sensational and romantic incidents.

If a cargo was to 'be worked' (sunk, and drawn up later) reports would be spread abroad of intended operations in an entirely different quarter to that where the run was to be effected; and if the Coastguard watch was too close to admit of a start being made unperceived two boats would be launched simultaneously and rowed off in opposite directions. The boat that was shadowed by the Coastguard galley would row away in a wrong direction, and after leading her chaperone a wild goose chase for a sufficiently long distance, would double back to where her consort was lying and help to work the goods. Strategy and cunning necessarily played a conspicuous part now in the successful prosecution of smuggling, and fortune did not always smile on the big battalions.

As the years rolled on, and the increased efficiency of the Preventive cordon put further difficulties in the way of the trade, the smugglers found it necessary once more to adapt themselves to this new environment. But the fates were against them – the trade was doomed and what, perhaps, tended more than anything else at this time to break the neck of smuggling was the strict enforcement of the 'limit laws', under which boats unprovided with a special licence, and if proved to be engaged in illicit practices, to condemnation followed by sawing the boat into three sections. The feelings, and language of the owner of a smart little vessel as he watched the source of so much profit being destroyed, can well be imagined.

As time went on, fortune declared more decidedly against the Cawsand men, and in the year 1879 the following memorandum was issued to the Coastguard Stations: 'In consequence of the large number of Cawsand and other boats taken, lost, and made to throw over their cargoes, the Coastguard are warned against the smugglers employing French boats.' The implication of this was that if they chartered a French boat, the Revenue cruisers had no power to interfere with it while out of territorial waters. In these, the smugglers brought across their goods and sank them as usual in planned spots. By this cumbersome means the trade was continued for many years, with varying success, the 'working' and 'running' of the goods being carried out as before by the galleys, the backwaters running up to St Germans and other places behind Whitsand offering splendid opportunities for getting the goods safe away after landing. The whole coastline is riddled with caves and secret places, and there were plenty of friends always ready to facilitate the despatch of goods into the interior.

When the time came, not everyone in Cawsand was sorry to see the gradual demise of the audacious trade. An old man has left us his opinion recorded at the time:

It was a very good thing for the place that smuggling was put down, for it was the ruin of a lot of people, especially young fellows who served in the Navy, for, you see, in those days men only shipped for one commission, and when they came home again they wouldn't be over flushed of money; and finding smuggling going on briskly, they would take a trip across to France. If the goods were landed safe there would be grog going all night afterwards, aye, and all next day too for those who liked it; so it was difficult for a young fellow of spirit to keep out of the business, whether he intended to go smuggling or not. I can tell you this, though, none of the smugglers bettered themselves by it. There was an old saying that smuggling money never did any good to anyone. One moment there would be money and to spare, but it would all be lost later on; and every smuggler that I remember, died poor.

*

CAWSAND BAY

In Cawsand Bay lying, with the Blue Peter flying,
    And all hands on deck for the anchor to weigh,
We spied a young lady, as fresh as a daisy,
    And modestly hailing, this damsel did say –

'Ship ahoy! bear a hand there! I wants a young man there,
    So heave us a man-rope, or send him to me:
His name's Henry Grady, and I am a lady
    Arrived to prevent him from going to sea.'

Now the Captain, his Honour, when he looked upon her,
    He ran down the side for to hand her on board.
Cried he with emotion, 'What Son of the Ocean
    Can thus be looked arter by Elinor Ford?'

Then the lady made answer, 'That there is a man, sir,
    I'll make him as free as a Duke or a Lord.'
'Oh no!' says the Cap'en; 'that can't very well happen;
    I've got sailing orders – you, sir, stop on board.'

But up spoke the lady, 'Don't you heed him, Hal Grady;
    He once was your Cap'en, but now you're at large:
You sha'n't stop on board her, for all that chap's order!' –
    And out of her bosom she drew his discharge.

Said the Captain, 'I'm hanged now, you're cool, and I'm
        banged now!'
    Said Hal, 'Here, old Weatherface, take all my clothes!'
And ashore he then steered her: the lads they all cheered her:
    But the Captain was jealous, and looked down his nose.

Then she got a shore tailor for to rig up her sailor
    In white nankeen trowsers and long blue-tailed coat;
And he looked like a squi-er, for all to admi-er,
    With a dimity handkerchief tied round his throat.

They'd a house that was greater than any first-rater,
    With footmen in livery handing the drink,
And a garden to go in, with flowers all a blowing –
    The daisy and buttercup, lily and pink.

And he got eddication befitting his station,
    – For we all of us know we're not too old to larn;
And his messmates they found him, his little ones round him,
    All chips of the old block from the stem to the starn.

Old Ditty

*

One morning in the autumn of 1895, a liner dropped anchor
in Plymouth Sound. She had come from the London docks
with 160 passengers, and was here to pick up a few West
Country ones. Her name was *Emmaville II*, and she was on the
way to Australia, powered by steam-engine and sail; and the
round-the-world voyage would take about twelve weeks.

Two of the passengers were relations of mine, my grandfather Richard and his wife Caroline. They were waiting for a boat to take them from Cawsand Bay to the waiting liner. Richard had already been round the world five times and on each he kept a diary. I have already in a previous book made this voyage with Richard but we've never been further than Honolulu. This time, by magical means, we are about to share his experiences at and after Honolulu on his way to cross America from San Francisco to New York and home. I hope my readers will find the sharing of this traveller's journey (with generous business expenses) as interesting a venture as I do, to see how things were for travellers a hundred years ago.

This was a business trip for Richard who was head of an engineering firm in Birmingham which had agencies all over the world.

Even in these days of aeroplanes it would be quite something to have done that.

'We arrived off the entrance to Honolulu harbour in good time,' writes Richard. 'We were offered a glass of wine in warm and beautiful sunshine on the boat deck. I thought of little Cawsand, now lying magnetically upside down to us, far, far away and hoped she didn't know.'

Just before they were about to land, one of the passengers, in the darkness, fell overboard, but being a good swimmer and a strong man he managed to get aboard again.

This gentleman, [writes Richard,] had the reputation of being something of a sceptic, and that afternoon I had been discussing the subject of a future state. When he was safely on deck again I reminded him of our conversation, and asked what were his thoughts when under the water in such a perilous situation. He replied, 'I will tell you exactly what I did think. When I fell overboard I had three shillings in my hand, and my first thought when under the water was as to their safety: so, before doing anything else I safely deposited them in my pocket and then proceeded to try and climb out.'

On landing, they found themselves amongst a motley crowd with faces too dark to be seen, but the majority dressed in light coloured raiment, and all laughing, shouting, jabbering and shrieking in a ten times more lively manner than a mob of, say, Neapolitans on the arrival of a train at Naples.

They found the hotel about a mile from the landing place, and very much enjoyed the walk along the wide unpaved streets lined with houses of curious shapes and sizes, many with gardens around them. Myriads of flies lit up the darkness, while the air was laden with the perfume of tropical flowers.

On arriving at the hotel they found it to be a spacious, well lit building with lofty reception rooms through which they wandered in search of waiters to whom they could give orders for supper, but no servant could they find, nor could they get any response to the bells which were vigorously rung by a hungry crowd. They made their way to the office, and were there informed they could not get anything to eat until the morning as the servants had 'gone home' and nothing was served after nine o'clock. It was in vain they declared they were starving, the only reply they could get was what they liked to drink at the bar. A Yankee standing by, pitying their plight, said it was quite true they could get nothing that night, but told them how they could be first to be served in the morning. He recommended them to order their breakfast at the office before leaving, and to pay for it there and then, and to be at the hotel again before seven o'clock in the morning. This they did, and then they returned to the vessel where they also were too late to have anything to eat.

In the morning [recalled Richard] we were punctually at the hotel buying some delicious strawberries on the way, then on finding our way to the breakfast room we were informed we could not obtain admission until seven o'clock. At the appointed hour the folding doors were opened by two natives and we were seated at the tables which were crowded with a bountiful supply of most tempting viands, and with quantities of luscious fruit.

As soon as all the seats were occupied the waiter closed the doors and was most assiduous in seeing that his staff attended to the wants of the guests. Presently there were wild knockings at the doors to which no attention whatever was paid, and when the knockings were varied, with hungry exclamations from our friends outside, the waiter's face became blander and blander. When we were quite finished (and I fear, we were in no hurry to depart) the doors were opened to admit a further batch of impatient voyagers, and even then, only one half of the expectant throng could be admitted; the remainder were advised to betake themselves to the restaurants in the town. We shall not forget our experiences at the Honolulu Hotel, the landlord of which is none other than His Most Gracious Majesty, the King of the Huvian Islands.

We occupied the remainder of the limited time at our disposal in walking and driving around the town and neighbourhood. On passing the Post Office it occurred to us to ask if there were any letters (though we did not expect any). Putting our cards on the table we said we supposed there were no letters for us. 'Oh, but there are though, and I'll be very glad to get rid of them,' said the clerk, whereupon he produced a huge packet of letters and papers, to our intense delight.

Richard judged the natives a fine lot of people, wonderfully lithe and active and with dark flashing eyes. The women of the labouring classes were very stately-looking, and walked with a dignity and grace a duchess might have envied. Their clothing was not very extensive in character, consisting apparently of one long, loose robe, gathered neatly around the neck and wrists with gay-coloured ribbons, suggesting the idea that seven years would be an unnecessary time for a Honolulu girl to be bound to learn dressmaking.

They met a number of little girls coming from school, and asked them to show them their books. At first they were very shy, but when he showed them a new three-penny piece, they came forward willingly enough, and one little girl called Emma, after the good queen of that name who visited England a few years since, read to them out of her school book in the true conventional schoolgirl monotone. They were greatly delighted to see Queen Victoria's face on the coins, and frequently repeated her name. The race was now fast dying out, and in a few generations would become extinct.

Honolulu to San Francisco

It was a beautiful moonlight evening, [records the diary] when we left Honolulu and set course for San Francisco, and after many months travelling by land and sea, we began to feel that we were at last really homeward bound, for would not our *next* voyage land us at Liverpool?

While at Honolulu a very considerable addition to our passenger list in the person of a number of Yankees, of both sexes, some of them being gentle folks and some not. We also took on board 3,000 bundles of bananas which were hung up in the netting all round the promenade deck. This was a most unfair arrangement on the part of the captain, as not only were the seats on this deck rendered unavailable, and a large portion of the space occupied, but the ship became over-run with centipedes, some of them five inches long, making it look like Egypt during one of the plagues for they were in all our quarters, in our beds and in our clothes.

The Americans, as a rule, are not good sailors, in consequence, I suppose of their bilious temperament, hence it is that when commencing a voyage they take it for granted that they are going to be ill, and make their arrangements accordingly. My companions had been flattering themselves that the spare berth in their cabin would remain empty to the end of the voyage, but they were doomed to disappointment, for it was their bad fortune to receive one of the most bilious looking of the new arrivals. On entering the cabin the first thing the Yankee said was 'Where d'ye throw up?' the answer to which was, 'We don't throw up at all, we *go* up and lean over the lee side.' Events proved the Yankee's apprehensions to be well founded. One party of the American men and women calling themselves gentlemen and ladies were returning from a long residence in one of the islands of the Pacific where they had acquired some of the native habits. One day, these people were taking their lunch on deck; it consisted of a native chicken dish called 'Pol'. This was a substance like bill-stickers' paste, and was contained in a large bowl. The company, which numbered some five or six persons, men and women, sat on the deck, and, having learnt from their new acquaintances to do without spoons and separate dishes, helped themselves to the delicious mixture by each putting two fingers into the common bowl until it was empty. They then attacked the chicken, and had evidently taken lessons in carving from the same authorities, for they adopted the primitive plan of pulling it to pieces. The captain had a large retriever dog on board, which had been eyeing the feasters for some time with the evident hope of being invited to join the party. Presently I observed one of the ladies call the dog, and having allowed him to take a bite, continued eating, and soon finished what was left, to the intense disgust of the noble brute. Of course, these proceedings excited considerable interest among the English passengers, but the party seemed quite insensible to observation.

One of our passengers was an American, named Steinberg, who had a grievance against the British Government, on account of an alleged outrage on the part of an English man-of-war's crew in some dispute in the Samoan Islands. He was nursing his wrath until he arrived at Washington, where he thought England's fate would be settled, and that she would be 'chawed up catawampously'. This man was accompanied by a Yankee journalist of a most anti-British type. He was a sallow-faced man with a large square lower jaw, without any hair on his face, and with straight, lanky locks, and, moreover, was something under five foot high [Richard was only five foot one]. He was so thorough-going in his hatred of everything British that when 'God save the Queen' was sung at the close of a concert in the saloon, he got up and with much fuss stalked out of the room, followed by some half-dozen of his countrymen. On one occasion I heard a friend of this gentleman ask him if he had a chair on deck. He said he had not. I took the hint, and determined that, at any rate, he should not use mine. Soon afterwards it happened that a sea breaking over the deck soaked the carpet seat of my chair, which obliged me to place it in a sunny position that it might dry. Presently I saw this newspaper man deliberately fetch the chair, which was a very comfortable one, and taking it into the shade, settle down in it. I went to him and remarked that the chair was quite wet. His only reply was 'I guess it's dry now,' with the peculiar twang of a down-east Yankee. Seeing that he failed to take the hint I told him that the chair was mine, and that I would thank him to give it up. This he did, with a remark that 'he did not see why people who were always walking about wanted any chair at all'.

The arrival of the ship at San Francisco was a most moving occasion. Richard wrote of it thus:

We sighted the magnificent harbour at daybreak on a beautiful morning at the end of April [1880], and when we approached it the sun had just risen, bathing the whole scene in a flood of golden light, fully justifying the name the Golden Gate. In a short time the city came into view, reminding me, surprisingly, of Sheffield, from the dense masses of smoke which hung over a large part of it.

Soon, they were boarded by a motley crew consisting of Custom House Officers, hotel touts, porters, agents for the railway, and a number of keen-eyed gentry desirous of earning a cent, any way, honest or otherwise.

They decided to stay at the famous Palace Hotel, and having found an agent, placed the luggage under his care – receiving checks for it. They locked their cabin and proceeded ashore, where they found the most sumptuous omnibus Richard had ever seen waiting to take passengers to the hotel.

San Francisco

'What an immensely splendid building,' said Richard as they drove up to the hotel, 'are we quite sure it's for us? There's nothing so grand as this, even in London!' And, certainly, he was not understating the grandeur of the hotel, for it had more than 1,000 bedrooms, rarely unoccupied by all of a thousand inhabitants, including some servants living in the house [this was 1880, remember]. The establishment had its own gasworks and a first rate fire brigade, also a magnificent artesian well affording an abundant supply of the purest water. Also present was its own squad of police. The rooms on the ground floor were twenty-five feet high, and corresponding size, the walls being hung with excellent copies of the best works of the great masters. The corridors were paved and lined with white marble, and the grand staircase was of the same white marble. There were no less than five hydraulic lifts for the conveyance of guests and luggage to each floor of the house.

The bedroom of this splendid hotel were very large and airy, and they all had comfortable dressing-rooms attached, with hot and cold water supply and with a dozen beautiful towels of all shades, forming a very refreshing sight to the traveller who had been cabined and confined for the previous month in the limited space allotted to passengers on an ocean steamer.

The bedrooms had baths adjoining, each bath being arranged for two rooms: there was also a service room on each landing, where a dusky negro was always in attendance. The dining-rooms were very spacious and fitted with a large number of small tables for parties of from four to eight people, an arrangement very much superior to the long tables in most *salles à manger*.

There were some 400 waiters, one-fourth only being white men, the rest negroes. The latter seem especially adapted for waiting, being active and nimble, and seeming to anticipate every wish. A fresh bill of fare was printed daily for each meal, and the variety of each meal was great, there being a choice of *about seventy* dishes at dinner. In the kitchen were twenty-seven French cooks, besides assistants, forming a sufficient guarantee for the excellent manner in which the food was prepared.

There was too, a splendid laundry in the house where the washing was done by fifty Chinese women; and certainly never was more linen more exquisitely got up. These Chinese were especially successful in all kinds of starching requiring a smooth polished surface such as shirt fronts. The way they applied the starch was quite novel, for having taken a mouthful they blew it out on to the article in a continuous fine spray, while their hands were occupied in ironing!

The servants took their meals from the *table d'hôte* menu, being waited upon by a batch of their fellow servants, and 'everything is conducted with the greatest possible regularity and order'. Richard was much pleased to find that all the gas and water system, also the hydraulic lifts and pumps, were supplied by English manufacturers, and were such as to command the admiration of everybody.

The day after we arrived at the hotel [wrote Richard] I was surprised at receiving a letter in a most familiar style, and commencing, 'Dear T —, If you should wish to see me you can do so by calling at my office, No. — Montgomery street between 10 and 5. My wife is dead.'

The name was quite strange to me, so I decided not to go and sent a friend. My friend found the address which was a wretched room at the top of a lofty pile of buildings, and after a few minutes' conversation with the man he found there, he was very glad to get into the street again, not liking the aspect of things.

Next day, whilst seated at dinner with my friends, a waiter came to ask which of us was Doctor L —. On being told, he said a messenger from the Chief of Police was waiting to see him.

Richard looked at the doctor and asked, 'What have you been doing?' Having finished dinner, they adjourned to the office and found the officer who said his chief had received a telegram from a man in some town 100 miles away, inland, requesting him to send 'his friend the doctor up to him as soon as possible.' 'Of course, my friend, knowing nothing whatever of the man, declined to go up country.' Later Richard mentioned these attentions to a gentleman who was dining at the same table.

He told me it was a favourite dodge with sharpers. On the arrival of ocean steamers it is the custom to publish the names of the passengers in the evening papers, which accounts for the familiar style adopted by these people in addressing strangers.

We had amusing chats with that lawyer. He said to me one day that I must have met with a deal of 'characters' in travelling: 'Yes,' I replied, 'I had, both good and bad.' He replied, 'Waal, I guess it's better to meet with bad rather than none at all.'

The Chinese are very numerous in San Francisco, there are more than 10,000 there. At the time of my visit the feelings of the rowdies ran very high against them, and threats were freely used against them of wholesale massacre. John Chinaman is a most industrious, frugal man, spending very little upon his living, and nothing upon his pleasures, always excepting his infatuation for opium. His needs being few he can afford to work for very small pay, and thus comes into competition with the white workman. While the workmen have their own special grievances about the Chinese, the wealthy classes have theirs, too. It is true that 'John' does his master's work well and cheaply, but, as I have said before, he is not a spending man; his sole object is to get, what the Yankees call, 'a little pile' as quickly as possible and then return to his native land.

The Chinese quarter is full of interest, the people swarming like bees, live in an appallingly crowded state. The butchers' and barbers' shops are the most numerous and the most interesting, the former being filled with a quantity of dreadful-looking little portions of meat, but it would puzzle the most learned to say from what animal they were cut. On looking at them one could not help thinking of what one had read of the fate of bow-wows and mew-mews in China. The barbers' shops are situated in the basement of houses, with an open front towards the street, and they are very numerous, for the Chinese are close shavers!

On looking down you may see a number of men seated in a variety of positions, each one smoking a pipe of opium, while the barber is occupied in shaving every portion of his head and face, excepting, of course, his beloved pig-tail. The swell Chinese is very particular and every hair shall be removed, and so clever do the operators become that, by means of tiny razors, they can shave the inside of the nose! Some of the pig-tails are of enormous length, and sometimes the white rowdies attack the Chinese and cut off their pig-tails. When a man has an especially fine one, he either rolls it up at the back of his head and fastens it with hair-pins, or else tucks it inside his blouse. I noticed one of the latter, in particular, employed a novel way. The owner had evidently let down his back hair before putting on his shirt, and consequently the pig-tail, which disappeared at the back of his neck, emerged from under the shirt and extended down to his heels.

The Chinese are accused of having brought with them a number of objectionable practices, but to anyone possessing a knowledge of the lower classes in American cities, it will appear not at all possible that the Chinese can be any worse than they are.

Most of the traffic in San Francisco is carried on with the use of tramways, and it may not be out of place to put intending visitors on their guard with respect to a little peculiarity in their arrangement. It is advisable to tender the exact fare, if possible, for if you give a larger one the balance is returned to you, not in cash, but in tickets available for future rides, which you may not have any opportunity of taking. The hackney carriages are very fine, being almost equal to English private carriages. Most of these I saw were splendidly horsed with a pair of magnificent animals, generally black. The lowest fare taken is ten shillings, but I am bound to say you can have full value for your money in the time and accommodation they give you.

On Sunday morning the city presents a very lively aspect. The Fire Brigades and Volunteers parade the streets, preceded by their bands, and thousands of people go by tramway and other vehicles to see the famous sea lions at the entrance to the Bay.

Across America
Richard and Caroline lingered in beautiful San Francisco for a fortnight. Two weeks' enjoyment of the comfort and good fare at the Palace Hotel made them fearful they were getting too

luxurious in their habits; but their friend, the lawyer, remarked they need have no fear on that account, as the fare on the Pacific Railway would cure even the severest attack of gout.

In order to get good seats in the train going east across the Continent, it was necessary to make arrangements a few days before starting. Tickets were obtainable at a score of places in the city; and in order to save all unnecessary trouble with the luggage during the long journey, sufficient for use in travelling had to be separately packed, and the remainder handed over to the Baggage Master who had an office in the hotel and who gave checks in exchange, undertaking to deliver it at any hotel or railway station in New York or any other place they might desire. By attending to this overnight they saved themselves immense trouble. It avoided them having to join in the confused scramble in the terrible heat and dust the following morning. They felt great relief when the train began moving out of the station when they felt that at last they were really starting on their ride across the Rocky Mountains.

The route through Sacramento Valley lies across agricultural land, teeming with richness. In many cuttings through which the train passed the soil was twenty feet deep, and the corn, which in many cases was over ten feet high, was fast ripening, and its glorious golden colour often charmingly varied by immense patches of marigold in full flower. Soon after leaving Sacramento the ascent commences, and the next day the party had good views of the deserted Californian gold diggings which first made California a household word throughout the world.

Richard found that life on board a Pullman train was almost more peculiar than that on board ship. His party were fortunate enough to secure a cabin partitioned off from the rest of the carriage, but the remainder of the sleeping berths had no partitions, being separated only by curtains. Inexperienced travellers were inclined to forget this and sometimes caused much amusement in consequence. One morning he heard a young lady complaining to her mamma that she could not find her stockings, a remark eliciting numerous offers of assistance from all parts of the carriage. A neighbouring compartment was occupied by a lady and a gentleman, the former of whom was deaf: with the peculiarity often observable in deaf people she imagined everyone else was deaf, too; the consequence being there were no secrets in that cabin!

Every carriage had a negro attendant whose duty it was to make the beds and to attend to the ladies' and gentlemen's lavatories, the ladies and gentlemens being placed at opposite ends of the carriage. At half-past nine, Sambo began to prepare the beds, and soon after ten almost everyone had retired, and as fortunately there are no decks to be paced, sleep soon comes for the weary. Arrangements were made for three meals a day, the train stopping at stations convenient for the purpose, and notice being given half an hour before. Half an hour was allowed for each meal, the invariable charge being a dollar.

As the train stopped, a general stampede was made for the dining room, the position of which was unmistakable, for at the door stood a negro with a face devoid of expression, vigorously sounding a Chinese gong. As each person passed in he paid his dollar, and made a rush to the end of the room where the cook was usually stationed. Happy was he who possessed a long arm and a quick eye and a silent tongue was likely to come out with much less than a dollar's worth. The experienced traveller, before sitting down, gathers all the dishes before him and proceeds to attack them all at once. As soon as the half hour had been reached, the guard called out with a shrill, nasal twang 'All aboard!' and we once more continued the journey.

Englishmen travelling in the States were particularly struck with the thin reedy quality of voice peculiar to Americans and the almost entire absence of the full deep-chested tones of German and Englishmen.

The Pacific railroad was single track, and although a wonderful engineering work was not by any means a substantial or confidence-inspiring line judged by English standards. The rails were old and worn, the bridges and viaducts were lightly constructed, and were almost always of wood. It was not to be wondered at that awful accidents sometimes occurred. The train which they were travelling in narrowly escaped falling down into a ravine 120 feet deep. It was on one dark night when everyone had retired to bed when they were awakened by continuous whistling and ringing of bells.

It was in vain that we enquired of the guards and attendants as to what was going on, for they, like their brethren all the world over, would give us no information. One thing, however, they could not hide from us, for we found we were being taken across a viaduct one carriage at a time, and as we crossed we could see lights moving about at a great depth below. On arriving at Omaha two days later, we found a full report on the occurrence.

It appeared that the viaduct had been discovered to be in an unsafe condition, some of its timbers having been partially burnt, and it was a matter for discussion whether the crossing of the train should be allowed at all. Richard's was the last train that went over, for before daylight the whole structure fell with a tremendous crash. The Indians were on the warpath at the time, and it was supposed that the work of destruction was theirs. The railway runs through some of the most magnificent scenery in the world. Sometimes its course lay through narrow valleys, or canyons, where there is just room for the railway and the river, sometimes through immense pine forests, and then again on a mere shelf cut in the face of the granite mountain until the point called 'Cape Horn' was reached. This was the turning point between East and West, and soon after the greatest elevation was attained, 8,200 feet.

About sixty miles of the more exposed portion of the road was covered with sheds to protect it from the snow. This result was not attained without considerable discomfort to the passengers, as the carriages became filled with smoke and dust while passing through.

One of the passengers on our train was an old man who had not crossed the country since he went out to the far west some twenty years before – long before the railway had been thought of. The party with which he was travelling was so large that it had to be split up into detachments for the convenience of pasturage. One night, his section had been attacked by Indians, who killed several of the party and drove off with most of the horses and cattle. The old man had for many years been a trapper in the Indian country, and had invested his hard-won earnings in a lot of horses which he was then taking out west, for the purpose of trade, and he was not proposing to lose them all at one fell swoop without making a bold dash for their recovery. His plan of operation had been soon settled, and in the evening he had set off in pursuit with half a dozen picked men, each with his rifle and a good store of ammunition.

After some hours they had come upon the scent of Indians, and moving cautiously forward amongst the scrub, presently saw them around their fires busily engaged in dividing the spoils of the morning. The trapper being a first-rate marksman, it was agreed that he should do all the firing, while the others loaded and handed up the rifles as fast as required. Every shot told, and the redskins, judging from the rapid firing that the whole party of white men were upon them, made a regular stampede, leaving horses and cattle and other spoils behind them.

For about a thousand miles the railway is open to the prairie without any enclosure, the consequence being there are frequent accidents occurring through cattle straying onto the track. I counted more than twenty carcases of these unfortunates in one day, and on one occasion, while sitting on the steps of the Pullman car, I felt a sudden check, and immediately after the body of a cow flew past. The herds are looked after by men with lassoes, riding very fleet horses.

The American railroads being much less protected from stray animals than those in England, the locomotives are provided with an apparatus called a 'cow-catcher', which consists of an iron framework projecting in front and inclined downwards as near to the ground as possible. The contrivance is successful in moving most living obstacles from the track – for instance, when a cow gets between the rails and sees the train approaching, it becomes dazed, and the iron frame striking the lower portion of its legs takes it up readily; but with a bull it is quite different; when his lordship sees the enemy approaching, he puts his chin down upon his fore feet, and awaits the onset with a confidence not by any means always misplaced. In this position his head and feet form a wedge which, becoming inserted beneath the iron frame, frequently throws the engine back on the train, causing serious accidents. When at Ogden, I saw the remains of a goods train which had been wrecked in this way the week before, the engine-drivers being killed. Also killed were two stowaways who had secreted themselves under the carriages. Little Cawsand, indeed, was a long way away.

II

Whitsand Bay
(*Near Plymouth*)

Wherever you stand on the cliff edge of Whitsand Bay, you stand on a gentle curve with Gribben Head and Dodman Point to the west, and Rame Head to the east. Though the curve is a shallow one it is large enough to embrace smaller bays within its extended circumference, bays such as Looe Bay, Portmadler Bay, and then around a bit further Talland Bay and Lantivet Bay, and Lantic Bay. The cliff face is a magnificent sight, stretching for some twenty-five miles, clothed in greenery from top to toe, down to the jagged black ribs of rock, all but buried in the copious area of near-white sand and pointing, menacingly at the incoming waves.

This beach has a sombre record for shipwreck; time and time again in contrary winds, fine ships and little ships, ocean-going and coastal, trying to beat up the Channel, tacking into merciless winds that forced them to become embayed, were entrapped in the bay, forced on to the lee shore and driven aground. There follows a few of the tersely framed announcements published in Lloyds List at the time:

November 13 1861: The smack *Diligence*, from Looe to Par, with lead ore. Sunk yesterday.

19 February 1867: The *Preciosa* from Skien, with timber, in entering the harbour caught the ground and filled. The water is partly over her decks.

November 24 1870: The ship *Belmont*, from Rangoon, Falmouth, to Liverpool.

An example of the dangers involved for participants

appeared in the *Naval Chronicle* of 1798 which, under date of 27 December has the following item of news:

> Last night, about ten o'clock, Humphrey Glynn, an officer of the Customs belonging to a boat stationed in Cawsand, whilst in the execution of his duty, was shot by a party of smugglers. He died instantly. The boat in which he was killed was commanded by Mr Ambrose Bowden who, together with the deceased and three other officers, fell in with a very large smuggling cutter about three miles south of Whitsand, which was lying at anchor. She was just about to put her cargo of brandy into boats, then alongside her, preparatory to landing on the beach of Whitsand Bay.
>
> When Mr Bowden got within hail of the smugglers he told them what his boat was – one of the Customs' – upon which they immediately fired point-blank into her, and repeated the fire many times, the second and third of which struck the deceased and carried away the whole front of his head; and then he dropped and expired immediately. The fire was returned from the boat and kept up so gallantly that the smuggler cut her cable and put to sea without landing her cargo.

So far, at any rate, the fortunes of the day, or rather of the night, were with the smugglers. Their ship, the *Lottery*, then disappeared from the scene; and we hear of her next only through another item of news in the *Naval Chronicle*, 18 May 1799: 'Arrived at Plymouth, the *Hinde* revenue cutter, with the *Lottery*, smuggler, having on board 400 ankers of spirits. She threw overboard 200 ankers in the chase.' [One anker was a 2-gallon cask.]

The subsequent trial of the crew of the *Lottery* supplies details which embellish that bald account. It appears that the revenue cutter *Hinde*, commanded by Captain Gabriel Bray, was cruising off Start Point; and on 13 May 1799, at about 3p.m., observed a large cutter, presently identified as the *Lottery*, making for the shore. As soon as the smuggler observed the *Hinde*, she altered course and put about for Bolt Head to the westward. Chase was maintained throughout the night. By five o'clock next morning, the two vessels were off the Lizard, some five miles apart, when their further progress was stopped by a calm; whereupon Captain Bray sent two of his boats, duly armed, and under the command of the mate, Hugh Pearce, to take possession of the smuggler. The revenue flag was hoisted on the *Hinde*, and a gun fired. As the boats drew near the smuggler, the crew were desperately trying to row the vessel away, using long sweeps [oars]. A gun was fired at them, and a man was calling through a speaking trumpet to 'keep off them boats immediately!' The mate of the *Hinde* then rowed up to within a cable's length of the smuggler, when he was again warned that if the boats did not keep off they would be fired upon and sunk. He stood up and shouted to them that they were the *Hinde*'s boats, and that he had orders to board the vessel; orders he must obey. He further added that he knew their vessel. It was the *Lottery*, and that he knew the men on board. Someone aboard rejoined that they cared not a damn who the boat belonged to, or who happened to be in it, that the vessel was not the *Lottery*, and that unless the boats kept off they would be fired upon, and all of them killed. The mate observed that the vessel's name on the stern had been covered up with canvas. He also observed that during these parleyings three guns had been run out and that a man with a musket was ready to fire. Bearing in mind the fate that had overtaken Glynn, five months earlier, in dealing with these same desperate men, he thought it prudent to withdraw.

The boats had not long returned to the *Hinde* when a breeze sprang up. Both vessels made sail, but the revenue cutter, proving the faster, and gaining on the Lottery, convinced the smugglers that it would be prudent to throw much of their contraband overboard.

Still the *Hinde* gained, and at two o'clock in the afternoon off the Longships [Land's End] her chase-guns were brought to bear. Observing this, the smugglers shortened sail, lowered their boat, and twelve of them jumping in, rowed as fast as they could for shore.

The two boats of the *Hinde* were then sent in pursuit, and captured them half-way. At the same time, the *Lottery* herself was taken, with five men on board, and with a cargo comprising 716 ankers of gin and some tea and tobacco.

The *Lottery* instead of, as was often the case, being condemned and destroyed, was taken into the Revenue service and performed some smart work on her new commission. Thus we read, 'October 25th, 1799. Plymouth: came in the *Lottery* [now a revenue vessel] with the *Assistance*, smuggler, from Guernsey, with a sunken cargo which the *Lottery* had gallantly got out of Whitsand Bay.'

The majority of the smugglers of the *Lottery* had meanwhile been tried and sentenced, but there remained the more serious affair of the killing of Humphrey Glynn in the previous December to be disposed of. Roger Toms, in some degree implicated in it, was among the captured smugglers, and 'to save his life' as he expressed himself, gave an account of the affair, implicating among his comrades William Searle, Thomas Ventin and Thomas Potter. On the charge of wilful murder they were brought up at the Old Bailey, on 20 December 1799; but the principal witness, Roger Toms, with King's evidence, could not be found. He had been mysteriously spirited away, as the prosecution stated, from the custody in which, for his own safety, he had been kept aboard. (This was on a revenue cutter in Fowey.) Application was therefore made, and granted, to postpone the trial until he could be found.

It turned out that he had been lured ashore and hidden in a cave on the coast by his neighbours and associates still at large, and was eventually conveyed to Guernsey. There he was on the point of being smuggled over to America, when he succeeded in making himself known to the revenue officers, and so was rescued and produced as a Crown witness at the trial at the Old Bailey on 10 December 1800.

The evidence is interesting. It appeared that the night of the two-year-old tragedy was one of brilliant moonshine, and that all the unloading operations of the *Lottery* could be distinctly observed. When the revenue boat was seen approaching, the smugglers hailed the boat to keep off or they would be fired upon. Bowden replied that he was a Revenue officer, and they could fire if they pleased. He then stood up and unfurled the Revenue flag, whereupon the smugglers made good their promise and opened fire. When three shots had been fired Bowden saw the oar fall from the hand of the second man, and called to him, not thinking that he had been hit, to 'mind what he was about.' The bowman then exclaimed 'Glynn has been shot!' Bowden, taking up a musket, returned the smugglers' fire, which in turn was quickly returned. The *Lottery* then cut her cable and escaped. Glynn was found to be dead.

Toms deposed that he was a mariner aboard the *Lottery* cutter on the night in question. Their cargo consisted of spirits, and they had just despatched several boatloads to Cawsand, when he went below. While between decks he heard voices cry, 'Keep off' and 'It's a King's boat!' There was then firing and presently orders were given to cut the cable, and they then ran before the wind to Polperro.

A conversation then took place between the master and Potter, Searle, and another, the former saying, 'He should be sorry if any harm had taken place in the firing,' and Potter replying that 'he had taken good level when he fired, and was sure he saw a man drop.' Toms said further that at the time the firing took place, Ventin, the cook, was sent below into the cabin by Oliver, to make the pokers red-hot with a view to firing the swivel guns, if necessary; and that after the cable had been cut he went on deck and heard Searle say that 'he was glad the boat had been kept off; that he had fired, but meant to do no harm, and hoped he had done none.

Searle and Ventin were acquitted but Potter was convicted and hanged at Execution Dock.

We are lucky to have had left to posterity the *Autobiography of a Cornish Smuggler* by Harry Carter who roamed the seas some 200 years ago between Brittany and Cornwall with 'tubs' of brandy and wines, each cargo of which was illicit and which therefore invoked the possibility at the end of the passage, of a hazardous game of men and guns between crews to be played out. The length and the rough, rocky features of the Cornish coast with its numerous caves provided plentiful opportunities for avoiding contact with the Preventive officers, though each landing was always a dangerous business.

Harry Carter tells of an awkward experience that befell him

soon after his young wife had borne him a daughter. He had gone on a cross-channel trip to Guernsey to bring back a cargo of spirits and tobacco. This was quite a normal trip for him, but to us, reading today of its composition in terms of armament makes one catch one's breath: for the vessel he used was a lugger of 140 tons (45 tons in today's measurement) mounting as many as sixteen carriage guns.

After making one voyage home to King's Cove in Mount's Bay 'I got a cargo for Cawsand, and as I depended on them people to look out if it were of any danger, according to their promise,' came into Whitsand Bay. After some time he came within hailing distance of a boat from Cawsand, and learnt that it was a 'clear' coast and there was no danger for him to bring his vessel there to anchor where they should have enough boats for him to discharge all his cargo immediately.

On hearing this intelligence, Carter brought the vessel to anchor, leaving the jib and the mizzen and trisail set, and

I began to make ready, opening the hatches etc. when I saw two boats rowing up from the shore. I said to the pilot, 'There is two boats coming to take the goods out', and soon after one of them came alongside, and the man in the bows asked me if I knew 'these was two man-o'-war's boats?'

Harry Carter immediately cut his cable, and before the stranger gathered headway it was right under the stern. One of the crew cut off the mizzen sheet, another, with a musket shot, shot off the trisail tack and boarded over the stern.

My people [said Carter] having some muskets, dropped them down and went below. I, knowing nothing of that, thought that all would stand by me. I began to engage them as well as I could without anything in my hands, as they took us by surprise so suddenly; having my greatcoat about me, I seeing none of my people, only one man at the helm; and when they saw that no person opposed them, they turned upon me with their broad swords, and began to beat away upon my head. I found the blows very heavy – crushed me down to the deck – and as I never lost my senses, rambled forward. They still pursued me, beating and pushing me so that I fell down on to the deck of a small raft just out of their way. I suppose I might have been there a quarter of an hour, until they secured my people below; and then found me lying on the deck. One of them said, 'Here is one of the poor fellows dead.' Another answered, 'Put the man below.' He answered again, saying, 'What use is it to put a dead man below?', and so passed on.

About this time the vessel struck ground, the wind being about East SE blowing very hard right on shore. Harry lay very still for about two hours hearing the talk of the boarders as they walked by him. The night was very dark on this 30 January 1788.

Another man was ordered to take the 'dead man' below, after which the commanding officer gave orders for a lantern and a candle to be brought. They lifted up one of Harry's legs as he was lying on his belly; he let it go, and it fell as dead down on to the deck. The officer then put his hand up under his clothes, between his shirt and his skin, and then examined his head, and so concluded saying, 'This man is so warm now as he was two hours back, but his head is all to atoms.' Ever since this experience Harry Carter has marvelled what a miracle it was he never sneezed, coughed, or drew breath that they perceived in all that time, not less than ten to fifteen minutes.

The water now being ebbing, the vessels began making a great heel toward the shore; it was only a little time after that, as their two boats were being made fast alongside, that one of them broke adrift. Immediately, there were orders given to man the other boat in order to fetch her. Harry, seeing the confusion, took advantage of it:

I thought it was time to make my escape so I crept on my belly on the deck, and got over a large raft just before the mainmast, close by one of the men's heels, as he was standing there handing the trisail. When I got over the lee side to swim on shore in a stroke or two, and as I was lifting myself over the side, I was taken with the cramp in one of my thighs, and so then I thought I should be drowned. However, I was still willing to risk it, so that I let myself over the side very easily by a rope into the water, fearing my enemies would hear me. I let go, and as I was very near the shore, I thought to swim on shore but I found myself sinking like a stone; and hauling astern in deeper water, I gave up all hopes of life, and began to swallow some water.

I found a rope under my breast, so that I had not lost all my senses. I hauled upon it and soon found one end fast to the side just where I went overboard, which gave me some hope; and then, with a final struggle I felt my feet touch bottom. As soon as I could, I attempted to run and immediately fell down; as I fell, looked round about me and saw three men standing close by. I knew they were the man-of-wars' men looking for the boat, so I lay there quiet for some little time, and then creeped upon my belly I suppose about the distance of fifty yards; and as the ground was scuddy, some flat rocks mixed with channels of sand, and fearful of being seen creeping over it I made the second attempt to run, and fell in the same manner as before. My brother Charles being there, looking out for the vessel, desired some Cawsand men then to go down and see if they could pick up any of the men dead or alive. I was not expecting to see any more, and once again fell to the ground. One of the men saw me and ran to my assistance, and taking hold of me under the arm said, 'Who are you?' So as I thought him to be an enemy, I made no answer. He said, 'Fear not, I am a friend, come with me,' and then there came two more who took me under both arms while the other pushed me in the back, and so dragged me back ashore.

By now completely exhausted, Harry was taken by them to a room where there were seven or eight men and to his great joy his brother Charles. They immediately stripped him of his wet clothes, and one of them pulled his shirt off and put it on to Harry. They sent for a doctor and put Harry to bed.

I went over in my mind the events of the day, and many a

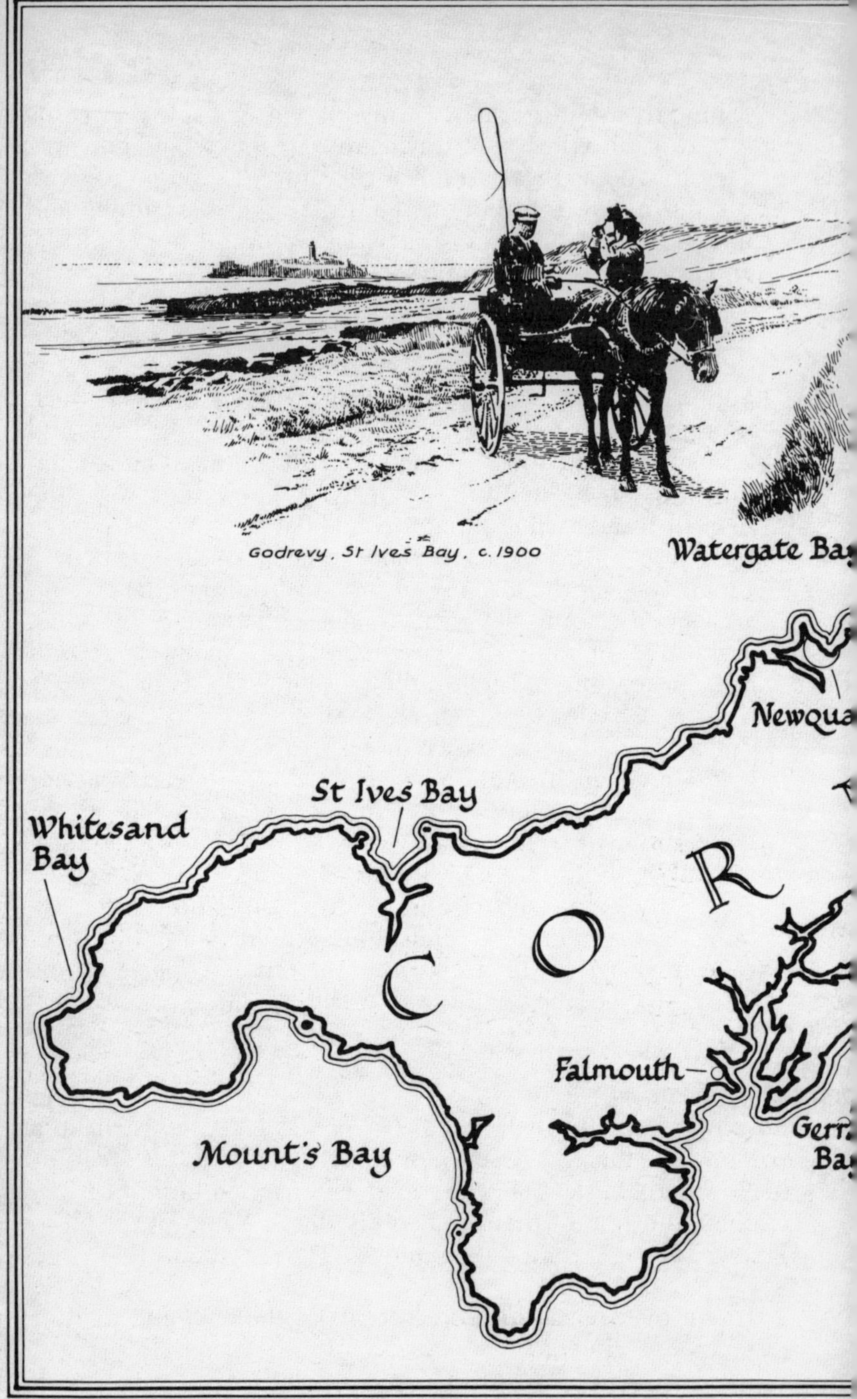

Godrevy, St Ives Bay, c.1900

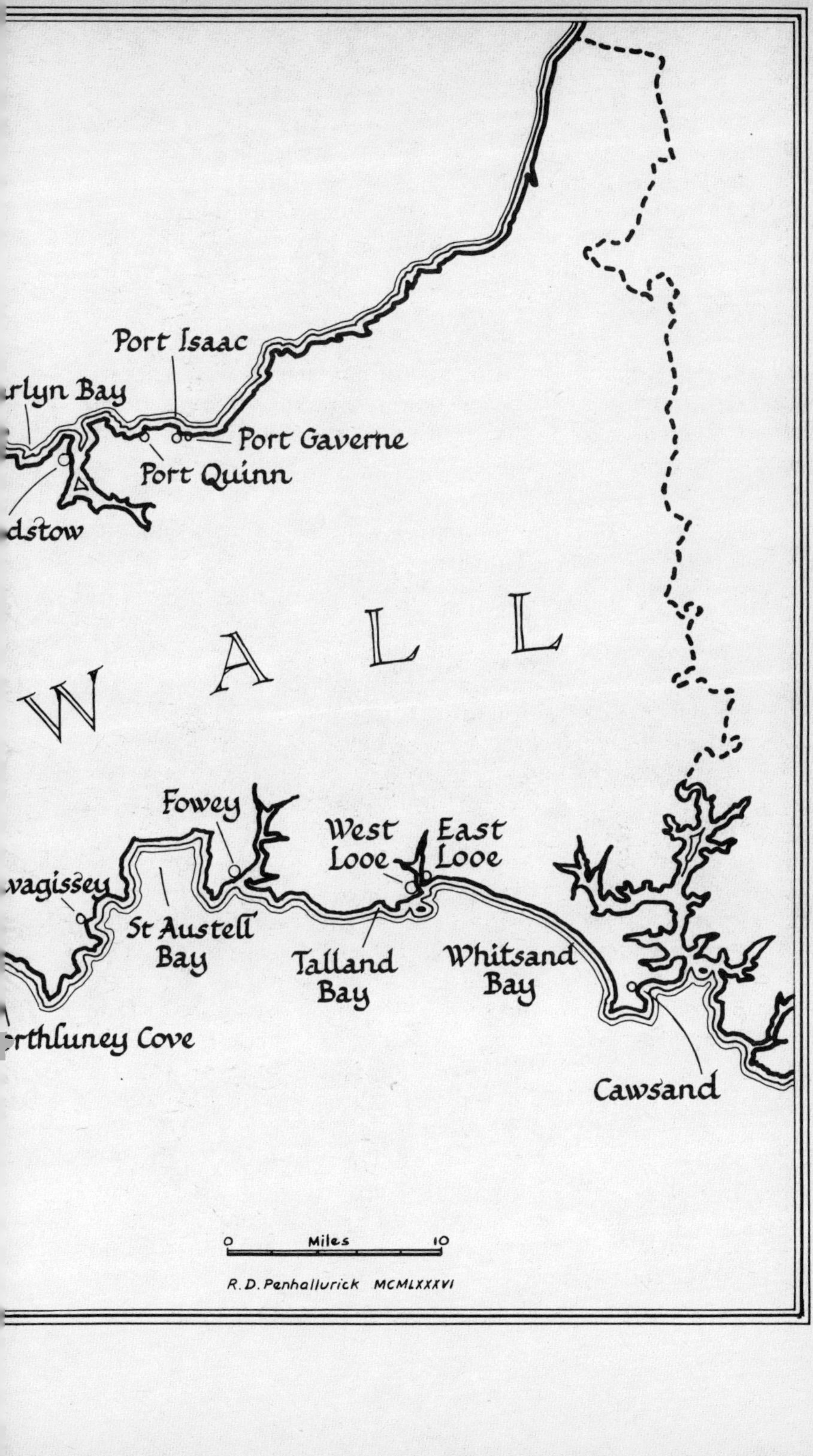

Port Isaac
rlyn Bay
Port Gaverne
Port Quinn
dstow
W A L L
Fowey
West Looe
East Looe
vagissey
St Austell Bay
Talland Bay
Whitsand Bay
rthluney Cove
Cawsand
Miles
0   10
R.D.Penhallurick MCMLXXXVI

time since then, what a wonder it was. The bone of my nose cut right in two, nothing but a bit of skin holding it, and two very large cuts in my head that two or three pieces of my skull worked out afterwards; and after so long lying on the deck with that very cold weather, and being not altogether drowned, but almost I think, I did not know I was wounded or lost any blood.

And now, we hear for the first time Harry's reference to religion which henceforth was going to be the major factor in this smuggler's rough life, leading, paradoxically one might say, to his conversion.

Now [Harry writes] I am going to show you the hardening nature of sin. When I was struggling in the water for life I gave up all hope: in my mind I was dead: nevertheless my conscience was so dead asleep I thought nothing about Heaven or hell or judgement; and if I had died I'm sure I would have awak'd amongst devils and damned spirits. See here this great salvation and that of the Lord. I have been very near drowned, I think, twice before this, and have been exposed to many dangers many a time in the last five years, privateering, smuggling etc., but I think conscience never so dead as now.

I stayed there that night and the next evening took chaise [public carriage]. My brother and me, and the doctor came with us as far as Lostwithiel, and arrived at home the night after at brother Charles' house. I stayed there some six or seven days, until it was advertised in the papers that three hundred pounds would be paid for the apprehending of the Captain, for three months from the date thereof, which set us all of alarm. So I moved from there to a gentleman's house in Marazion. I stayed there about two or three weeks, and from there moved to Acton Castle as my brother John rented the farm, the family not being there then, so that the keys and the care of the house were left to his charge, and after a few days went back to Marazion again. I used to half-burn my coals by night in order that there should be no smoke in the daytime.

In the course of about three months, when my wounds were nearly healed, I used to go at night to the King's Cove, and there to drink grog etc.

This mention of King's Cove leads me to leave the Carters for a while. We have seen their life-style imposed on potentially peaceful little Cawsand Bay, and we will meet them again when we come to visit, in due course, Mount's Bay where the lively Carters had their base.

III

Looe Bay

There are three small bays next to, and to the west of, Whitsand Bay that are full of character, and with a varied experience that belies the innocent-sounding name, Looe Bay. We will leave the long sloping face of high cliffs, cloaked in greenery, that is Whitsand, and turn our attention westward to these smaller bays, none of which, I may say, relinquishes a hunger for wrecks.

The bay adjacent to Whitsand is Looe, taking the delightful name from the town. Its character has been formed in part by such diverse ingredients as fishing, coast trade, smuggling, the fact that there is not one Looe but two, East Looe and West Looe, and a hundred years ago ... well let's learn from a contemporary of the 1850's of the lifestyle that was reflected in the waters of the bay.

Wilkie Collins tells us that Looe existed as a town in the reign of Henry I and remained one of the prettiest and most primitive places in England. The river divided it into East and West Looe, and the view from the bridge looking towards the two little colonies of houses, thus separated, made it in some aspects unique. Looking down from the hills you could see the houses of the town straggling out towards the sea along each bank of the river in mazes of little narrow streets; curious old quays projected out at different points; coastal trade vessels loaded and unloaded, built in one place and repaired in another, all within view, while the prospect of the hills, the harbour and the houses thus bound together was closed at length by the English Channel just visible as a small strip of water, pent in between two promontories which stretched out on either side of the beach.

That is what Looe looked like from a distance in the 1850's, and it lost none of its attractions when you looked at it more closely. Incidentally, there was no such thing as a straight line in the place. No house had fewer than two doors leading into different lanes; some even had three, opening at once into a court, a street and a wharf, all situated at different points of the compass.

The shops, too, had their diverting irregularities, selling all and everything. Here you might call a man a Jack of all Trades, as the best and truest compliment you could pay him.

Viewed from the town the bay was very small and formed by the extremity of a hill on the right and jagged black slate rocks on the left. A massive pile of large rough stones had been built as bulwark to the incoming seas. It was here that the young and the old were drawn to lounge and gossip, keeping a look-out for any outward bound ships seen in the Channel, and to criticise the appearance and glorify the capabilities of the Looe fleet of fishing boats riding snugly at anchor before them at the entrance of the bay.

There were fourteen hundred inhabitants in Looe, the women taking much of the hard work out of the men's hands. 'They are as good-humoured and as unsophisticated a set of people as you will meet anywhere' was Collins' conclusion. Women were constantly seen carrying coals from the vessels to the quay in curious hand barrows. They 'laugh, scream and run in each other's way incessantly; but these little irregularities seem to assist rather than impede them' was Collins' conclusion.

As to the men, all they were interested in, it seems, were the boats, for the whole day long they were mending boats, painting boats, cleaning boats, rowing boats or, standing with their hands in their pockets, looking at boats.

The children seemed to be children in size, and children in nothing else. They congregated together in sober little groups, and held mysterious conversations. If they ever did tumble down, soil their pinafores, throw stones, or make mud pies, they practised these juvenile vices in a midnight secrecy.

Until the Reform Act was passed in 1832, Looe sent no less than four Members to Parliament. This was before the one man/one vote law superseded that of the 'rotten' boroughs when a seat could be bought. Here is an example of how, in one case, this was done. It concerns the 'election' of one of these four members.

On the morning of the 'Election', one division of the borough sent *six* members, electors, and another four to record their 'imposing' aggregate of votes in favour of any two smiling civil gentlemen who came, properly recommended, to ask for them. This done, the ten electors walked quietly home in one direction, and the two members walked quietly off in the other to perform the fatiguing duty of representing their constituents' interests in Parliament. And now to something quite different.

About a mile out to sea, to the south of the town, a triangular shaped edifice rises above the blue waters. It is Looe Island. Here, at the end of the eighteenth century, a ship was wrecked. The crew were saved, so were several passengers, unwelcome passengers. These were the ship's rats who had somehow managed to flee from the vessel in favour of taking up residence on the island.

In the process of time those rates increased and multiplied exceedingly, there being every prospect of destroying the island's potential. It was therefore appropriate for the people of Looe to make a determined effort to extirpate the whole colony of invaders. Ordinary means of destruction had failed to have effect. It was said that rats left for dead on the ground had mysteriously revived faster than they could be picked up and skinned, or flung into the sea.

All the available inhabitants of Looe joined in a great hunt. The rats were caught by every conceivable artifice; and once taken were instantly and ferociously *smothered in onions*. The corpses were then decently laid out on clean china dishes, and straightway eaten with vindictive relish by the people of Looe. Never was any invention for destroying rats so complete and so successful as this. Every man, woman and child, who could eat, could swear to the death and annihilation of all the rats they had eaten. The local returns of dead rats were not made by the bills of mortality, but by the bills of fare; it was getting rid of a nuisance by the unheard-of process of stomaching a nuisance.

Day after day passed on, and rats disappeared by hundreds never to return; what could all their cunning and resolution avail them now? They had resisted before, and could have resisted, still, the ordinary force of dogs, ferrets, traps, sticks, stones and guns arrayed against them, but when to these engines of assault were added, as auxiliaries, smothering onions, scalding stew-pans, hungry mouths, sharp teeth, good digestion and the gastric juice, what could they do but give in? Swift and sure was the destruction that now overwhelmed them – everyone who wanted a dinner had a strong personal interest in hunting them down to the very last. In a short space of time the island was cleared of the usurpers. Cheeses remained entire; ricks rose uninjured. And this is the true story of how the people of Looe got rid of the rats.

Wilkie Collins leaves us a delightful picture of Looe on a day of festivity, on boat-race day. In addition to a boat-race there was to be a bazaar on the beach; and as fine weather was therefore an essential requisite on the occasion, it is scarcely necessary to report that it rained unusually heavily. In the forenoon, however, the sun shone with treacherous brilliance; and all the women in the neighbourhood fluttered out in his beams, gay as butterflies. Dazzling gowns, flaring parasols and joyous cavalcades on cart-horses were to be seen on the road leading to the town, and a mixture of excitement, confusion, anxiety and importance possessed everybody, but, alas, as soon as the gun fired for the first race the clouds began to muster in ominous blackness, the deceitful sunlight disappeared, and the rain came down for the day – steady, noiseless, malicious rain that at once ruled out any hope of clear weather.

Dire was the discomfiture of the poor ladies of Looe. They ran hither and thither for shelter, in lank, wet muslin and under dripping parasols, displaying in the lamentable emergency of the moment all sorts of mysterious interior contrivancies for expanding around them the exterior magnificence of their gowns, which never ought to have been seen.

Deserted were the stalls of the bazaar, for the parlours of the alehouses; unapplauded and unobserved, strained at the oar the stout-hearted rowers of the boat-race. Everybody ran for cover, except some seafaring men who cared nothing for the weather, some inveterate loungers who would wander up and down in spite of the rain, and three unhappy German musicians, who had been caught in their travels, and penned up, tight, against the outer wall of a house, in a sort of cage of canvas, boards and evergreens which hid every part of them except their head and shoulders. Nobody interfered to release these unfortunates. There they sat, hemmed in all around by dripping leaves, blowing grimly and incessantly through instruments of brass.

If the reader can imagine the effect of three phlegmatic men with long bottle noses, looking out of a circle of green bushes, and playing waltzes uninterruptedly on long horns in a heavy shower, he will be able to form a tolerably correct picture of a large extra proportion of gloom which the German musicians succeeded in infusing into the gloomy proceedings of the day.

The tea-drinking was rather more successful. The room in which it was held was filled to the corners, and exhaled such an odour of wet garments and bread and butter (to say nothing of an incessant clatter of china and bawling of voices) that we found ourselves as uninitiated strangers, unequal to the task of remaining in it to witness the proceedings. Descending the steps which led into the street from the door – to the great confusion of a string of smartly dressed ladies who encountered us, rushing up with steaming kettles and craggy lumps of plumcake – we left the inhabitants to conclude their festivities by themselves, and went out to take a farewell walk on the cliffs of Looe, our thoughts pondering on the fate of the island now clearly visible out to sea.

This scene had been dampening in more ways than one, but, at least, there wasn't a storm, which would have been dramatic, but unwelcome. We have an eyewitness account of the cruel vigour of a storm from that splendid Cornish author, Jonathan Couch, who was a native of Polperro, a Looe Bay town, too:

In the time of a storm Polperro is a striking scene of bustle and excitement. The noise of the wind as it roars up the valley behind the town, the hoarse rumbling of the angry sea, the shouts of the women and children carrying tidings of the latest disaster are a peculiarly melancholy assemblage of sounds, especially when heard at midnight. All who can render assistance are out of their beds, helping the sailors and fishermen; lifting the heavy boats out of reach of the sea, buffeted by the storm, blind in the wet darkness, or taking the furniture of the ground floors to a place of safety. When the first streak of morning light comes, bringing no cessation to the storm, only serving to show the desolation it has made, the effect is still more dismal.

The wild fury of the waves is a sight of no mean grandeur as it dashes over the peak and falls on its jagged summit, from whence it streams down the sides in a thousand waterfalls and foams at its base. The infuriated sea sweeps over the piers, and, striking against the rocks and houses on the warren side, rebounds towards the strand, and washes fragments of houses and boats into the streets, where the receding tide leaves them strewn in sad confusion.

It was terror which fell on Cornish fisher houses when the October storms rose along the coast. No one who has witnessed it can ever forget the sight when the people stood huddled together on the cliff-top in driving rain, watching the boats vainly trying to make the harbour, while every time the boats were hidden by the trough of tremendous waves, the women's shriek was heard above the pounding roar of the storm, while the men stood silent.

Another threat to the livelihood of those who lived on this part of the coast, from Rame Head to Fowey, and further, was the fear of a visit from the pressgang who were the main source of supply of men for the Navy.

These pressgangs knew that on this coast they were entering a large storehouse of the finest fighting material that could be wished for the Navy. Consisting of some dozen men or more, they would descend upon a town or village and, in the name of the King, seize hapless seamen without so much as a warning, and take them swiftly away from their homestead and deliver them to the nearest Yard for a long period of service in warships. The men of this area lived close to danger as seamen, who knew no other occupation; and their experience of smuggling, for example, an example of coping with danger, was fine training for service in the Navy. Yes, their daily trade was to encounter dangers to be fought off.

IV

Talland

Talland, midway between Polperro and Looe, was a favourite spot with the daring Polperro men. It offered better opportunities than those given by Polperro itself for unobserved landings, for it was, and still is, a weird lonely place, overhanging the sea, with a solitary ancient church well within sound of the waves below.

It was an easy matter to store kegs in the churchyard itself, and to take them inland, or into Polperro by the isolated, narrow country roads when opportunity offered, hidden in carts taking seaweed for manure to the fields.

At one time, Talland owned a sinister reputation in all this countryside, and occupants of the farmhouses told, with many a fearful glance over their shoulders, of the uncanny creatures that nightly haunted the churchyard: devils, wraiths, and fearful apparitions made the spot a kind of satanic parliament; and the accounts of these activities lost no accent or detail of horror by constant repetition, on dark winter evenings. This is not to say that other places round about were innocent of things supernatural; for those were times when every Cornish glen, moor, stream and hill had their bukkadhus, their piskies and gnomes of all sorts, good and evil; but the infernal company that consorted together in Talland churchyard was acceptable to these old-established creatures, who formed a class by themselves. People rash enough to take the church path through Talland after nightfall were sure to hear and see strange, semi-luminous figures, who were thought of then as being betokened to the evil and benificent reputation owned and enjoyed by Parson Dodge. This eccentric clergyman of

Talland was reputed to be an exorcist of the first order.

It was Parson Dodge who, doughty wrestler with the most obstinate of species, found himself greatly in demand in a wide geographical area for the banishing of troublesome ghosts for a long term of years to none other than the Red Sea. It was also claimed that he controlled a number of diabolical lackeys who resorted nightly to the vicarage to do his bidding. The village and surroundings thought that, to revenge themselves for this servitude, this group lurked in the churchyard and got even with mankind by pinching and smacking and playing all manner of tricks on who dared to pass this way under cover of night. One Uncle Jack Chowne even got a black eye on one dark night when, coming home along this way under the influence of spirits not of supernatural origin, he met a posse of fiends and, in the amiable manner of the truly intoxicated, insisted on them adjoining with him to the nearest inn, 'just for the shake of ole timesh'. In fact he made the sad mistake in taking the 'fiends' in question for friends, and addressed them as friends, even by name; with the result that he got a sledge-hammer blow in what a prizefighter used to call 'the peeper'.

If he had adopted the proper method to be observed when meeting spirits, i.e. if he had stood up and said his password, 'Nummy Dummy', all would doubtless have been well; this form of exorcism being in Cornwall of great repute and never known to fail.

But the real truth of the matter, as you, my reader, must have by now realised, was that those savage spooks and mischievous shapes, were really youthful, local smugglers in disguise engaged concurrently in a highly profitable nocturnal business, and in taking the welcome opportunity thus offered in an otherwise dull circle of establishing a 'rag'.

Parson Dodge himself was something more than suspected of being of the spooks, for Talland was, in fact, the scene of many a successful 'run' that could scarce have been successful had not this easy-going cleric amiably permitted it.

It is thus peculiarly appropriate that in this lonely churchyard we can see today an epitaph upon one Robert Mark. It is a tragic enough epitaph, its tragedy disguised, perhaps, by grotesque little cherubs carved on the headstone. Here is that epitaph:

Robert Mark
late of Polperro, who Unfortunately was *shot at sea* the
24th day of January in the year of our Lord God
1802 in the 40th year of his Age.

————

In prime of life most suddenly
  Sad tidings to relate
Here view my utter destiny,
  And pity, My sad state:
I by a shot which rapid flew
  Was instantly struck dead
Lord, pardon the Offender who
  My precious blood did shed.
Grant him to rest, and forgive me
All I have done amiss;
And that I may rewarded be
  With everlasting Bliss.

Robert Mark was at the helm of a boat which had been obliged to run before a revenue cutter. It was at the point of escaping when the cutter's crew opened fire upon the fugitive, killing the helmsman on the spot. He had been one of the crew of the *Lottery* in the affair of 1799, and had served a term of imprisonment in connection with it. He had, in fact, only recently been released. The mild and forgiving terms of the epitaph, surely that of a devout Christian, is most unusual alongside the other epitaphs in the cemetery. The usual run of sentiment to be seen on the considerable number of these memorials to smugglers cut off suddenly in their youth is not so magnanimous. For instance:

In memory of Thomas James, aged 35 years,
who, on the evening of the 7th of December, 1814,
on his returning to Flushing from St Mawes in a boat
was shot by a Customs Officer and expired a few days after.

Officious zeal in luckless hour laid wait
And wilful sent the murderous ball of fate:
James, to his home, which late in health he left
Wounded returned – of life is soon bereft.

V

Fowey Bay

Fowey is one of the loveliest of Cornish ports, and Fowey Bay one of the most historic.

If you are lucky enough to be there on Club Regatta Day, the beauty of the bay is enhanced by the silent approach of yacht after yacht of exquisite line, making her way to moorings in the centre of the hill-surrounded harbour, sheltered from malevolent winds. But Fowey has often had to partake in events of violence that have brought terror to the town, and grief for the bay which has been the unwitting aid to enemy incursions. Yet that has not always been one way. Richard Carew, of Antony, tells us that in Edward III's days

sixty tall ships did belong to this harbour and that the town of Foys did assist the King with forty-seven sail of men-of-war and transport-ships in 1347 in order to reinforce the siege of Calais; whereupon the King granted commissions to the chief commanders of those Foy ships to take French prizes during his wars with those people, so that in a few years those Foy men were grown so rich and formidable by taking French prizes [keeping the capture for themselves] that by force and arms they would enter many ports of that kingdom, and carry with them all ships they could conquer, and what they could not, would use means to set them on fire in the places where they lay.

In fine, when French prizes grew scarce they scrupled not to turn sea-robbers, or pirates, taking, plundering, and destroying all ships they could master, of what country so-ever, not sparing the sailors' lives. By which means the townsmen grew unspeakably rich and proud and mischievous, which occasioned the Lord Premier, and other Normans, to petition John, King of France, to grant them a private commission of marque and arms, to be revenged on the pirates and thieves of Foy town, which accordingly they obtained, and carried their design so secretly that a small squadron of ships, and many bands of marine soldiers, were prepared and shipped without the Foy men's knowledge or notice, who accordingly put to sea out of the river Seine, in the month of July, 1457, and with a fair wind, sailed thence across the British Channel, and got sight of Foy harbour, where they lay off in the Bay till night, when they drew towards the shore and dropped anchor. In the night they landed their marine soldiers and seamen, and at midnight approached the south-west end of the town where they killed everyone they met with, set fire to the houses and burnt half of them to the ground.

This was retribution indeed for their 'piratical practices'. Women and children did not escape the flames and the massacre but tried to escape into the hills.

Under the orders of John Treffrye Esquire the men grouped inside his newly built house, Plase [Place] where they stoutly opposed the assaults of the enemy, whilst the French soldiers plundered that part of the town which was unburnt, without opposition, till dark. The news of this French invasion flew far in the morning into the country, and crowds gathered together to raise the siege of the town. The Frenchmen, observing this, and fearing the consequence of a longer stay, having got sufficient treasures to defray the charge of the expediton, as hastily ran to their ships as they had deliberately entered the town, and as privately returned to France as they had clandestinely come into England, with small profit and less honour.

The townspeople besought the Earl of Warwick for help who

was very forthcoming with his sympathy and action taken. Being the Lord High Admiral he was able to grant some of the vessels new commissions for privateering and taking French ships (as prizes), on promise of 'their just and righteous proceedings, and renouncing the trade of piracy: whereupon in a few years they plied their sea business to such a degree that they began to repair and rebuild ruined houses.'

Alas, things did not quite work out as the Earl intended, for they soon fell again into their old trade of piracy, robbing and killing anyone they could beat. The King, Edward IV, hearing of this sent a messenger and serjeant-at-arms to Foy to apprehend some of those delinquents, and bring them up to London to be tried for those crimes, in order to receive condign punishment. But instead of obeying the King's command and officer, in contempt of his authority they barbarously cut off his ears and, so dismembered, sent him back to his master, the king, who wasn't going to be fooled again, so he sent down Commissioners to Lostwithiel under pretence of raising able seamen to go to war against the French, and that such amongst them as appeared most fit and able should have command of some of the King's best ships.

At this news a great part of the freemen and seamen of Foy were drawn to Lostwithiel; where they no sooner arrived but immediately they were apprehended and taken into custody, their ill-gotten goods and chattels seized by the King's Officers, and one Harington, a notorious pirate, executed.

The harbour of Fowey [wrote Carew of this period] abounds with deep and navigable waters for ships of the greatest size, overlooked by winding and lofty hills and, though narrow extends itself in several branches three or four miles up the country, and is navigable to Lostwithiel. At the mouth of the harbour are two small blockhouses the Polman and St Catherine's, and each is famous for a fight they had with a Dutch man-of-war of seventy guns, doubly manned, that had been sent from the main fleet of ships of eight sail, that lay at anchor. They had been in pursuit of our Virginia fleet – also about eighty sail – which had eluded the Dutch and had entered this harbour some time before. The Dutch had orders to force the two forts and to take or burn our Virginian fleet.

Accordingly, it happened, on that day, a pretty gale of wind blowing, this ship entered the haven, and as soon as she came within cannon-shot of the forts, fired her guns upon the two blockhouses with great rage and violence, and these made them a quick return of the like compliment or salutation. In fine, the fight continued for about two hours in which were spent some thousands of cannon-shot on both sides, to the great hurt of the Dutch ship, in plank, rigging, sails and men, chiefly because the wind slacked, or turned so adverse that she could not pass quick enough between the two forts up the river, so as to escape their bullets, but lay a long time a mark for them to shoot at, till she had the opportunity of wind to tack around, turn back, and bear off at sea to their fleet, to give them an account of their unsuccessful attempt and great damage.

After this engagement, the cargo of the whole Virginia fleet was landed at Foy (because its owners in London feared the hazard of the sea at the time of the Dutch War, to transport it there by water).

Nearly three hundred years later, Fowey was exposed to another enemy, and from a different armament altogether. Let us take a look into the autobiography of the author, Quiller-Couch to see the contrast. It is 1940:

I have been kept here [Fowey] on various duties, Fowey having become a garrison town with a bewildering number of units scattered around – R.F.A., R.A.F., R.E., some Yeomanry, half a battalion, not to mention the Navy – and myself, the one hardy J.P. sitting and representing Peace in the centre of the small cyclone ... A German broadcast the other day announced that Fowey was in flames.

We are all well here, by the mercy of Heaven and no thanks to the Boche. You haven't heard that the scoundrel dropped four heavy bombs on me the other day as I was working in my little orchard. No. 1 was a close call, striking the cliff some 20 feet away from me, and by the Lord's guidance sending the sherds straight up to scatter high over me as I fell on my face. No. 2 tore down a candle of cliffs, blasted a couple of oaks, and followed by No. 3 which removed an innocent crow's nest while No. 4 made a large crater, destroyed a smart brake dispersing the shale underneath it over some fifty yards. No. 4 fell harmlessly into the sea.

Bombs have ploughed up a field or two, with smaller bombs at the back of us hitting an empty schoolhouse, with some cottages at Polruan. But we go about our business surounded by the Navy and Army in large numbers, with cannon to the right of us and ditto to the left of us, a Bren gun in the next garden but one.

Noise everywhere has invaded this haven, speed-boat on patrol, gun practice – siren warnings, bombs, military cyclists hurrying to buy a postage stamp.

The foregoing is an example of history repeating itself, of Fowey experiencing violence from enemy attack in our time, just as it had formerly, as we have seen.

There is also a repetition of history repeating itself, then as now, in the line of commerce, when wars with France, lying just across the Channel, meant attacks at sea and deprived Fowey of safe trading. There is a delightfully relevant plaint on this. In 1810, the Reverend Richard Warner, on a walking tour, found Fowey experiencing

complaints of decay of commerce from the continuance of the war, and the shutting up of the Mediterranean trade. The stock of pilchards, the staple commodity of the place was decaying in the hands of the inhabitants ... When will that happy period arrive that shall behold the rulers of the world (anxious for the *happiness* of society), once more resting from the senseless struggles of ambition, giving some pause to the misery of mankind? When, considering *their own* proper *glory*, as identified with the prosperity of their subjects, they shall bid the sword of *war* rest in its scabbard and be still?

When the nations of the civilised world, hushed by their

fiat into *peace*, shall again exhibit that picture of tranquillity to which Christendom has long been a stranger? When their 'garners' shall be full and plenteous with all manner of stores; when their oxen will be strong to labour; when there shall be no decay, no leading into captivity, and no complaining in their streets?

Poor, chastened Fowey, now the epitome of peace for the holiday-maker, the yachtsman and the children has through the centuries lived in the shadow of anxiety. In 1620, nearly four hundred years ago, a Doctor Yonge, Fellow of the Royal Society, had this to say:

A very pretty harbour, hath a narrow going in but a great inlet. In the Dutch warr, a fleet of Virginia men saved themselves here, and some of them ran so far up the river as two or three miles. The town is very small, many ruined houses in it, hath a pleasant walk on the sea side from the town to the outpoint by ye way where there is an old castle which, at ye distance of about a hundred yards makes ye distinctest eccho I have ever heard, ye castle doth stand under ye hill on which ye walk is, and ye eccho perfect and distinct in ye space of few yards only.

Modern Fowey finds letting lodgings more profitable than fighting the French or Dutch, or beating off privateers. Relics of those days linger on either side of the harbour entrance in the ruins of two forts, from which a chain was stretched across to help repel an invader.

One cannot leave a visit to historic Fowey without a thought for two great families, the Treffryes and the Rashleighs who virtually owned the town through the last five centuries, the latter providing a Member of Parliament for many years. The Treffrye family still own Place in the centre of the town, but the Rashleighs are no longer there though Menabilly, their seat, still stands in sight of the sea, just west of Fowey overlooking St Austell Bay.

You and I, dear reader – if you are still with me – are now, in a few moments, going to make our acquaintance with John

Rashleigh of Penquite, and through him, or rather through his hitherto unpublished memoirs, we shall learn of the life-style of one of the Cornish gentry nearly two hundred years ago. I think we may find it surprising in its worldliness for one living so far from London town. But first, we shall take a look at the family business scene, at St Austell Bay.

VI

St Austell Bay

If you look at St Austell Bay on the map, flanking Fowey to the west, its very outline seems to suggest a sturdy presence, inviting activity, and disdaining the fun features of other bays. There has been a harbour opposite Menabilly, the seat of William Rashleigh, and another at Par to the north, and yet another at Pentewan (but now obsolete) to the south.

For a century and more one or other of these have been the outlet for the tin and china clay mines in the proximity, and for the delivery of coal.

Writing, in 1839, of the district, Cyrus Redding said:

There are several villages in this parish, but none save that of Charlestown, situated on Tywardreth Bay (a bay within a bay) is worthy of mention. This may be called the port of St Austle as it contains a pier for sheltering vessels, a basin, and a number of fishing boats, with a considerable trade. A large portion of the clay found near St Austle, called china clay, but really disintegrated granite, is shipped from thence to the manufactories in Staffordshire and other parts of the kingdom.

Near St Austle is the ancient tin mine of Polgooth. To the north-west of the town is a second singular tin work called Carclaze Mine which is open to the day. Nothing can be more dreary than the aspect of the earth's surface in these districts. The Carclaze Mine excavated out of a barren hill, looking like a huge punch bowl, a mile in circumference, is from twenty to thirty fathoms deep, and though it has been worked for 400 years, is still productive, and still enlarging its enormous circumference. The stamping of the ores is carried on within the mine.

The clay was identified as being fit for porcelain, by one Cookworthy, a chemist and potter from Plymouth. He recognised it as being the same as had been used for centuries by the Chinese. Somewhat naturally Cookworthy wanted to keep the secret to himself, but Josiah Wedgwood got to hear of it … The fascinating growth of huge pits and white clay mountains resulted in St Austell Bay working as an outlet to markets far afield. The Rashleigh name was henceforth connected with it, as was Treffrye, helping to build Charlestown harbour, just across the bay to Menabilly.

A constant problem that can be said to have diminished the business value that the mines in the district supplied was that a great accumulation of mud and gravel was washed from the mines into the Bay, silting up what otherwise would have been a good harbour. Par was abandoned in the 1840's due to insufficient depth of water for vessels to load or unload in.

It is sad that a beautiful bay like this one should have had to endure co-habitation with loads of gravel and mud that cannot fail to despoil the clear sea water. But now, here comes a Rashleigh.

Sir John Colman Rashleigh was born in 1772 at Penquite, in the parish of Golant (a little up river from Fowey). His father was the third son of Jonathan Rashleigh, of Menabilly, a name made famous in our time by Daphne du Maurier, and her book and film. We meet him through his unpublished memoirs which give a fascinating picture of the life of one born to a prominent family at the end of the eighteenth century.

'I come now,' writes Rashleigh, 'to the most eventful epoch of my life, my first quitting from a home which had been so happy and so improving, and my finding myself a mere child [1784], an utter stranger, at school.'

The school was the Grammar School at Lostwithiel, and there he spent, or wasted as he put it, 'five mortal years in it', being unable to look back on any redeeming circumstance. Incidentally, his mother was the daughter of the Reverend D.

Good, Headmaster of the Lower School of Eton College. The tenor of Lostwithiel Grammar School was somewhat different ... 'I am unable to look back on any redeeming circumstance for the prevalence of vulgarity, dirt, neglect and physical and moral degradation by which it was characterised.'

In fact, his schoolboy life began in utter misery, intensified by the warm and loving nature of his home environment hitherto. The contrast, the stark contrast, was unbearable:

Later, when I became familiar with the habits and practices of the school, and of the great body of its inmates, by degrees, I became thoroughly vulgarised, hardened and changed. It left me an ignorant and shallow smatterer, with no foundation laid on which it was suitable to erect the superstructure of a sound education.

It was true that among my schoolfellows, owing to the fashion of the days, there were a few gentlemen's sons, but they were few, and so far as I had means of judging, they very soon became assimilated to the great majority of those of whom the school was composed, and gave in to all the habits in which naturally they had been brought up; in fact, the taint thus contracted, did not only affect their manners and their learning, but communicated, as I shall ever be persuaded, a moral stain which no after experience could entirely eliminate.

Rashleigh at this point, with heavy emphasis, writes a splendid naively suggestive reference to the morals of the school. Much underlined, he writes:

I do not choose to be more plain on this most disgusting subject: I only mention this to be as a warning to those who may come after me that they expose not their sons, at the outset of their careers to the abominable contaminations of a low and vulgar school. A greater mistake cannot be made and it is singular that in the instance before me, so many parents seem to have been perfectly insensible to the consequence of such exposure.

The annual charge for boarding and teaching was, as

Rashleigh assessed, the paltry sum of eighteen pounds, an opinion we, in this day and age have no effort in agreeing; fourteen pounds of this sum was for board, and four for tuition. This brought the school within reach of all classes, yeoman and tradesman, besides the day boys who had the privilege of attending school gratis.

Of our master [writes Rashleigh] I wish to speak kindly, and as favourably as is consistent with the truth. He had graduated at one of the Scotch colleges. He was a man of fair parts and competent learning. With him, *at first*, I was a great favourite, and derived from him considerable improvement; but after a time this ceased and I was confounded with the herd and shared with them the neglect which, after a time, and when success had rendered him indifferent to his duties, we all suffered at his hands.

Through the intervention of a kind friend who had witnessed the effect on John of Lostwithiel school, his father was at length persuaded to take him away, and to send him to Chudleigh under the care of the Reverend John Garnett.

My summer holidays were spent in London [John goes on] with my brother. We took the Diligence to Exeter which started at five in the morning, proceeded all night and reached London the second day about three o'clock, p.m., that is, thirty-four hours.

Soon after my arrival in Russell Street where my father and mother were, my Uncle Young took me to see Lunardi ascend in his balloon from the open ground. [Now occupied by Russell Square; Vincent Lunardi, on 15 July, 1784, made the first ascent in a balloon over England.]

On this first visit to London John was taken several times to the theatre where he saw the famous Mrs Siddons, then in full blow of her reputation, in *The Mourning Bride*, *The Grecian Daughter*, and, last, in the character of Rosalind for her own benefit collection.

John Rashleigh's education, after his experience of the

Lostwithiel Grammar School, reached for greater heights than Lostwithiel could attain, and so he went to Eton, no small step up, one might say. He remained there four years, and at the end of it he described his life there as being a 'waste of time'.

It would seem that nature had bestowed a trace of his being an academic, albeit a minor one, for later he described his sojourn there as being 'a pleasant, but an idle life,' and his stay at Cambridge for two years that followed, as being also a waste of time. Later, perhaps he changed his mind about this for in 1799 he was called to the Bar, joining the Western Circuit.

And now, of the following year he writes, in tender fulsome style:

As the close of the year approached, the most important and, to me, the most auspicious and happiest epoch of my life, I was heartily tired of the idle, desultory life I had been having ever since my sojourn at Lostwithiel. I had also, at last, got my affairs in some order ... I had for some time meditated on, and put to the test, the constancy of her who afterwards became the wife of my bosom, the beloved mother of my children, and for thirty-four years the joy of my life, my best friend, my safest adviser, who had long honoured me by an attachment of which I was totally unworthy, but relying on which I was led to hope that I might at last, though undeserving of so great a blessing, succeed in my suit and form, moreover, a connection on every account peculiarly desirable, not only to myself, but to all those of my friends who were pleased to take interest in my happiness and wellbeing.

All was well, and John married Harriet Williams. They had a daughter, who died when only thirteen, much to the distress of her father.

The death of his father in 1803 was a great shock to John in more ways than one, for he died leaving very little money, and without a will. Making matters worse was the fact that his father, a gentle, loving man, had shielded his son from having anything to do with money, or the running of the properties on the estate. The way this now affected the family is related by John, thus:

> The year 1803 was not only an important epoch in my life, but on very many accounts was so serious a change in all its relation as to be, in fact, nothing less than a revolution. My father's way of bringing us up, shielded from the role of money, led us to be wholly dependent, and ignorant of the running of our own affairs.
>
> From the time I went to the Bar, my life had been one of privation, struggle, and temporary expedients, and but for the assistance which accident, in part, and the kindness of personal friends afforded me at times I should either have been plunged into degradation and despair, or have been tempted to break off, at every hazard that I faced, all connection with my profession. I took little or no thought for the morrow: and no-one had ever felt more unfit or worse prepared than I was, suddenly called upon, single-handed, to take upon myself a trust involving heavy responsibilities and deepest anxieties which their discharge and nature necessarily entailed ...
>
> My London life now seemed a long way away, but grateful I am to my father for the three years I spent there as an aspiring lawyer, years for which I now regretted I had not given my father the credit I owed him.

This debt comprised the opportunity to meet with many introductions which led to him meeting many 'of the most distinguished individuals in the ranks of London Society.' The contrast with Cornwall had always been in his mind while he acquired a knowledge of the world, as he puts it. He saw more of London life of every description and grade of character and reputation than otherwise he would ever have known; and he recalls the pleasures of knowing people of the theatre. 'I am indebted to a friend, one Charles Moore, for being introduced to a very different, and most agreeable, but, alas! to a young enthusiastic man such as I, a dangerous society – that of the Dramatic Corps in the theatre, and several of the Dramatic Authors'. Rashleigh then goes on to elaborate:

My friend, Charles Moore, to whom I owed this great gratification, for such it was, was not only intimate to those whom he introduced me, but with the whole Siddons and Kemble families – a pleasure I did not share with him. I still recollect, and ever shall, with the liveliest pleasure, the many most agreeable Soirees given by Miss de Camp, afterwards Mrs Charles Kemble, and mother of Mrs Butler and Miss Fanny Kemble at which I met, among others of public reputation and notoriety, Miss Pope, the accomplished sister of Mrs Clive, the Duchess of St Albans, then Miss Mellon, a beautiful and well-educated woman, Mademoiselle Parisot who, though generally only known as a danseuse, was, in fact, a highly and generally accomplished woman of remarkably pleasing manners; James Smith, an old acquaintance, and his brother, author of *The Rejected Addresses*; Mr Arnold, manager and proprietor of the Strand theatre; Miss de Camp's sisters, one of them the authoress of *Thaddeus of Warsaw*, another the actress mentioned by Charles Mathews in his account of his professional adventures, and a whole tribe of Literateurs, male and female connected with the theatre, and several men of fashion who were intimate with Miss Camp. To obviate the possibility of mistake I think it right to state that on the many occasions of witnessing the social manners of Miss Camp and her guests, I never saw the slightest deviation from the most perfect correctness, nor did I ever hear that our pleasant parties had been followed by anything inconsistent with the strictest decorum.

About this time I brought down a keeper from Hampshire, and at the same time several hundred brace of pheasants to try an experiment which, on every hand I was told was abortive, but which has perfectly succeeded, inasmuch as whereas there was not a single pheasant in the County west of Launceston, now they abound – more or less according as they are fed and preserved from that place to the very Land's End. I also hunted with my friends, R. Walker, and D. Stephens who had a pack of hounds, but the play of *Hamlet* was without its principal character, that is, they hunted foxes indeed but very rarely killed one.

My chief amusement became the breeding, rearing and selling blood or racing stock. For this, Mr Trevanion, my confederate, and myself, spared no expense at first, though he went on the turf regularly which I never did. I had the best advice and assistance from my friend Mr Weatherby, Editor of the *Racing Callender*. At this time also were established the Bodmin Races which, were it an honour to boast of, I was the founder. This fact, however, at the time, and until they died a natural death, none of those, high or low, who were in the habit of attending these Races seemed to remember, as I was never asked to become Steward in any one year. They were but dull affairs, and certainly did not, in any degree by the pleasure they afforded the Aristocracy, compensate for the mischief they did the population.

Rashleigh continued to reside at Lostwithiel from August 1803 to April 1808. 'Perhaps it was unreasonable for me to expect,' he muses, 'that a society such as this little town afforded would in any way accord with the habits and manners to which I have been used, and I have no doubt that my decision was right.'

On returning from London in September 1812, John attended many meetings in which he was concerned. He was also waited upon by a Deputation of the Electors of Fowey to request that he would stand for that place as by the death of his uncle the seat was vacant, and to give his answer on 3 October. Accordingly, he attended a public Meeting of the Electors in the Town Hall of that place. The seat was also to be contested by his cousin; and it was because of this that he declined the offer: on his return, his cousin 'came to me to express his sense of my handsome conduct':

In 1837 I did what I thought to be my duty. Having been invited to stand for Parliament, and having refused the invitation, I decided to do what I could to aid the Whig Party to gain the seat. Accordingly I set about getting involved in this political affray and found it a very expensive gesture. General extravagance in all polling districts, and if all the Bills sent in to us had been discharged in full, they would have amounted to a sum of not less than £5,500.

I have in another place, mentioned the treatment I received, in spite of remonstrance, in settling these Bills, as with the exception of Mr D. Stephens, and a worthy shipbuilder from Padstow, not one, gentle or simple, could be prevailed upon to meet and aid me; and therefore I solemnly resolved, and shall adhere to that resolution, never again to take a leading or responsible part in any future Election.

He did, however, continue to serve the community. Here, for instance, is an example of his duty to the Law:

> On 4 April a person, closely connected with Mr Charles Rashleigh's gamekeeper, was arrested under warrant issued by Mr Whindam, of Whindam, Lincs, upon a charge of burglary of a most aggravated nature. It was, of course, backed by me and entrusted to one of the Constables of St Austell parish. He succeeded in finding the man in bed with his wife, having been apprised that he was of a most desperate character, who had set at defiance the civil power at home. The man begged to be allowed to dress himself to attend the Constable, and that he and his party would leave the room as he did so. This was no sooner complied with than he sprang from his bed and jumped out of the window, and got clear off for a time, the Constable returning without him; but as an alarm was given, and the poor man was naked and utterly destitute, after being at hide-and-seek for a few days he had to surrender.
>
> He was then brought before me, secured, and sent with one of the Constables to Salisbury where he was tried, condemned and executed.

Unfortunately, we are not told of the nature of the burglary that led to the poor man's savage sentence.

On another occasion John attended a meeting of miners at Truro at which, to begin with, the High Sheriff presided. Its object was to prevent the duties on foreign ores from being taken off. The whole of the proceedings were assumed by Lord Falmouth, who not only moved the Resolution, but afterwards took upon himself what could only be described as a deposition of the High Sheriff, as he unceremoniously removed him from the Chair, and without a word of invitation occupied it himself. 'Never did I witness a more disgraceful exhibition of insolence on the one hand, and abject submission on the other.'

This worthy, kindly Cornishman, whose company we have enjoyed for a while, was made a baronet in 1837; and on this note, Sir John Colman Rashleigh, Bart, we bid you farewell and thanks.

VII

Mevagissey Bay and Port Luney

The coast line of Mevagissey Bay falls southward from St
Austell Bay, past Phoebe's Point, past Trenarren, Black Head
and Pentewan, pausing slightly at the stone work of Mevagissey
Harbour, and then displaying its passage along the golden
sands of Polkirt Beach, Colona Beach, Turbot and Great
Perhaver Beach.

Mevagissey is one of the Cornish fishing towns most noted
for the capture of the pilchard, a fish of great value to the
Cornish economy until the beginning of this century, and a fish
we will be giving some attention to a bit further on in this
book. Further to the west, fish and the potato formed the sole
nourishment of the poorer class, and in every little cove, where
it was possible, families living near contrived to keep among
them a boat for fishing, and thus they supplied themselves.
Mind you, there were many fish beside the pilchard that paid
them a call: for instance, the other side of Dodman Point, St
Austell Bay gives way to Veryan, a comparatively small bay
facing southward. In the north of this, and within its
boundaries, is a little cove, Port Luney, which is dominated by
a splendid building, Caerhays, which was the seat of the
Trevanion family, and now that of the Williams.

From time to time, a whale will arrive, from far away, off
Caerhays, or, I should say, several whales. The vicar, the
Reverend Wilmot, at the end of the last century informs us that
one summer there were several carcasses of whales floating in
the Channel. He asked a boatman whether he could account
for this. Speaking very deliberately he replied, 'The whales
have got the fever!'

The boatman, one John Banfield, was coming ashore one night at Port Luney about midnight, and instead of beaching his boat he ran it hard upon one of the whales which was sleeping in the shallow water. The upshot of it was that the whale dashed his boat into the air, filling the whole of the sea with phosphorescent light and chucking him into the bottom of his boat.

On another occasion there was the carcase of a whale floating about in the Channel and had been seen coming ashore with much fuss, whereas from the decayed state of its tail and hinder parts it must have been dead six weeks or two months. This carcase was towed round by the Portloe boatmen, its flesh and blubber cut up and boiled with the bones, and the oil raised some £100. As it was stranded on the beach, he stood upon its tongue and was not tall enough to reach the roof of its mouth.

Further down the coast, in Gerrans Bay, there is a visitor of a different kind, not quite so bulky as the whales in Port Luney but more in keeping with the environment. Writing in the year 1900, let Arthur Norway tell us the story. He begins by describing the shoreline:

Nowhere on this coast is the granite so rent and shattered, so split into spires and pinnacles and minarets and towering gigantic blocks of masonry, all of which, touched by the light wreaths of the sea mist which somewhere behind it has a hot bright sun, appear as unsubstantial as a fairy palace. Around the base of this superb medley of rock forms, the clear blue water laps and sparkles brightly. There is no living thing in sight save a single gull whose snowy plumage gleams as he skims the surface of the water, and again fades and disappears as he rises into the region of the mist.

It is singular good fortune that brought this weather, for in the struggling of the sun and the fog we can realise both aspects of this coast, so wildly beautiful and so steeped in fanciful romance, the tangled wreckage of a fierce and lusty life which was lived upon these shores more centuries ago than one can count. As mist flows around the headlands, little palpitating flashes are cast upon it from the hidden sun, so that the solid blocks and columns of granite appear to quiver, while out to sea, beyond the blue bay where the sun falls gently into a grey soft cloud, setting one's fancy working as the senses fail to pierce it or discover where it hides. Out of such a cloud might have sailed that spectre ship which haunts Porthcurno, the fine bay with a beach of lovely driven sand which lies a few minutes' walk away across the cliff.

Out of such a mist she always came, a black square-rigged vessel, sailing right up upon the beach, taking the sand without a shock or quiver, and pursuing her course steadily over dry land as on the sea, till she vanished in a smoke wreath higher up the valley.

There are several forms of the legend which accounts for the first coming of this ship; all centre on a stranger who came to dwell at Chygwiden up the valley; with a single servant, and who kept a boat at Porthcurno in which he and his servant put out to sea in the worst of storms. There was clearly something about these two strangers that awed the fishermen, but even tradition has forgotten what it was, and the tale remains a vague trace of former days almost as impalpable as the mist.

VIII

Falmouth Bay

Peaceful, law-abiding Falmouth Bay has witnessed only rarely expressions of unrest among the ships of the Royal Navy in its time. This was not so in other ports.

Falmouth was the station for frigates of the Channel Fleet patrolling the Channel and its approaches during the war with France at the end of the eighteenth and beginning of the nineteenth centuries. In command of the squadron was the brilliant Cornish admiral, Viscount Exmouth (Pellew) whose flagship was the *Indefatigable*. In less than four years, Admiral Exmouth had fought, and won, as many actions. By his seamanship and his example his ship's company was brought to a high state of discipline. In the language of an officer who served with him for nearly thirty years:

No man ever knew better how to manage seamen. He was very attentive to their wants and habits. When he was a captain, he personally directed them, and when the duty was over, he was a great promoter of dancing, and other sports, such as running aloft, heaving the lead, etc., in which he himself was very proficient. He was steady in his discipline and knew well the moment to tighten or relax. He studied much the character of his men, and could soon ascertain whether a man was likely to appreciate forgiveness, or whether he could not be reclaimed without punishment. During the whole time he commanded frigates, his men had leave in port, one-third at a time, and very rarely did a man desert.

His wonderful sense of leadership yielded wondrous results, as we shall see.

On one occasion when his ship, *Culloden*, was under easy sail off the coast of India, and preparations had been made for partially re-caulking the ship, a pitch kettle, full of hot pitch (which was against orders) on the fore part of the main-deck, caught fire, and immediately the ship was on fire.

Many of the crew jumped overboard, and others were preparing to do so when the sudden appearance of the Admiral allayed the panic. He ordered everyone to their quarters; the marines to fire upon anyone who should attempt to leave the ship; the yard tackles to be cut to prevent the boats from being hoisted out; and the firemen only to take the necessary actions for extinguishing the fire.

The captain, who was undressed in his cabin when this happened, received an immediate report of it from an officer and hastened to the quarter-deck. He found the Admiral calmly giving his orders from the gangway, the firemen exerting themselves, and the rest of the crew in their quarters, all as quiet and orderly as if nothing untoward had happened.

Early in the following year, the Admiralty decided to limit the period of command in frigates. This affected Sir Edward who, with much regret, had to leave the ship and *Indefatigable*'s crew he had for so long commanded. He was appointed to the *Impetueux*, the most beautiful, and probably the finest ship in her class of ship-of-the-line. He was permitted to select twenty of his men off the *Indefatigable* to follow him.

Going on board the *Impetueux* for the first time, he was accosted at the gangway by the boatswain who welcomed him with, 'I am very glad, sir, that you are come to us, for you are just the captain we want. You have the finest ship in the Navy, and a crew of smart sailors, but also a set of the greatest scoundrels that ever went to sea.' Sir Edward checked him on the spot, and afterwards, sending him to his cabin, demanded what he meant by addressing him in that manner.

The boatswain, who had served with him before on the *Carleton*, pleaded with his former memories as an excuse; and after submitting to the reproof with which Sir Edward thought it necessary to mark his breach of discipline, informed him that the crew were in all but a state of mutiny, and that for months past he had slept with pistols under his pillow.

Mutinies were the natural fruit of the conditions which had prevailed in the Navy, and it was only wonderful that discipline had been preserved for so long. Everything was supplied by contract, and the check upon the contractor being generally very inadequate, gross abuses prevailed. Officers who recollected the state of the Navy during the first American war could furnish a history that now would seem incredible. The provisions were sometimes unfit for human consumption. After having been long on board, casks of meat would be found uneatable. The biscuit, from inferior quality and a bad system of stowage, was devoured by insects until it would fall to pieces at the slightest blow; and the provisions of a more perishable nature, the cheese, raising, butter etc., would be in a still worse condition.

Among crews thus fed, the scurvy made dreadful ravages. The *Princessa*, when she formed part of Rodney's fleet in the West Indies, had two hundred men at the hospital at one time. The purser received some authorised perquisites instead of pay, and one-eighth of a seaman's allowance was his right, so that their pound was only fourteen ounces. Prize-money melted away as it passed through the courts and offices. Not even public charities could escape, and the noble Establishment of Greenwich was disgraced, by placing in it super-annuated servants and other landsmen, as worn-out sailors, and conferring the superior appointments, intended for deserving naval officers, or upon political friends.

A gradual improvement in all the departments of the public service began from the time of Mr Pitts' accession to power as prime minister, and the worst of these abuses had been corrected long before 1797.

Still so much remained that the demands of the seamen, when they mutinied at Spithead, were not less due to themselves only but for the general interests of the Navy. A moderate increase in their pay and Greenwich pensions; provisions of better quality; the substitution of trader's for purser's weight and measure; and an allowance of vegetables, instead of flour, with their fresh meat when in port, were their chief claims.

They did not resort to violent measures till petitions, irregular ones, it is true, had been tried in vain. They urged their demands firmly, but most respectfully, and they always declared their intention to suspend the prosecution of them 'if our Country should require our services to meet the enemy at sea.' However, though their claims were most just and their conduct, in many respects was worthy to be commended, it was a mistaken conclusion, and most deeply to be regretted. Hard as the principle may appear, no grievance could be held to justify a breach of discipline; and when the sailors at Spithead had placed themselves in the position of offenders, the question of redress ought to have been preceded by unconditional and, if necessary, enforced submission.

If the sailors had first been compelled to return to their duty, and afterwards their grievances properly investigated and redressed, the whole Fleet would have respected the authority which enforced obedience. As it was, almost every ship in the Home Station mutinied during the course of the year.

Sir Edward deeply lamented the submission of the Government. He was satisfied a proper firmness would have quelled the evil, and prevented it in the future, and he was strengthened in his opinion by the circumstances of the mutiny by one of the ships at Spithead, in which one of his own officers was a principal actor.

Captain Williams, of the Marines, formerly in the *Arethusa*, applied to his captain for authority to act, assuring him of the good disposition of his own men, and pledging himself by their actions to save the ship; but his captain, though one of the bravest and best men in the service, shrank from committing the marines to possible conflict with the sailors, and recommended a little delay. In a few minutes the Marine officer returned: it was not yet too late, but not another moment could be spared. The humane feelings of the commander compelled him still to falter, and when the marine officer returned, it was to say that his men must now save themselves, and the ship was lost. It was an example that showed that the more desperate mutiny at the Nore was not quelled by submission. At one time a mutiny was planned in Sir Edward's ship, *Indefatigable*, but he checked it before it broke out.

Indefatigable was lying, with the *Phoebe*, in Falmouth harbour, and the frigates were to sail the next morning when the crews determined not to proceed to their station in the Channel until they received their pay. A sailor who had overstayed his leave came in the dead of night to inform his commander of the plot. This came as a surprise to Sir Edward who might well have expected, being popular as he was, that a crew that had fought two successful actions within the past year, would be too proud of their ship and their commander ever to fail in their duty.

Determined to maintain his authority at all hazards, he prepared for the worst, and made such arrangements as he deemed necessary, now facing the possibility that he might have to face the dreadful necessity of a personal conflict with his crew. Things looked really serious when it was reported to him while the anchor was being weighed that the men were sulky and would not go round with the capstan.

Sir Edward, on hearing this, then came forward declaring his knowledge of their intentions, and he ordered the officers to follow his example. 'You can never die so well,' he said, 'as on your own deck quelling a mutiny; and now, if a man hesitates to obey you, draw your sword and cut him down!' The crew, accustomed to prompt obedience, and attached to their officers, at once returned to their duty and the *Indefatigable* was soon under sail, abreast of Black Rock and passing through the bay and out to sea. It was a calm day with cloudless sky and little wind, and the beauty of the scene belied the tension on board the ships.

Presently a boat was seen pulling from the *Phoebe*, and the captain came on board in a state of great excitement – his crew had mutinied! He begged Sir Edward to compel them to obedience. However, Sir Edward's plan for so doing had been turned down at Plymouth where making a severe example might have been useful, so Sir Edward felt unable to help, and Captain Barlow, unable to bring his men to their duty, had to allow his ship to sail eastwards from Falmouth and toward the company of the fleet and the mutineers. This was the last time that the fair bay of Falmouth tasted the taint of mutiny in the Royal Navy.

The crew of Sir Edward's ship, the *Impetueux*, supposed, and probably correctly, that Sir Edward had been selected to command them in consequence of their known disaffected state, his frigate having been almost the only ship on the home station which had not actually mutinied. Under this impression a mistaken pride would not allow them to be controlled, and their secret spirit of revolt became more determined.

The mutiny did actually take place later, in Bantry Bay (Ireland), and though the Falmouth experience is over for us, I feel that, having gone so far, my readers would wish to have a brief account of Sir Edward's experience of it; so I will bring to your notice a fascinating document, namely, 'A letter from Sir Edward Pellew [Exmouth] to Rear Admiral Sir Charles Cotton, applying for a Court-Martial on the mutineers of the *Impetueux*.' It runs:

>   *H.M.S. Impetueux at Sea, June 8, 1799*
> Sir,
>
>   It gives me considerable concern to be under the necessity for reporting for your information the extraordinary and unprovoked mutinous conduct of a great part of the ship's company of his Majesty's ship under my command, on Thursday, the 30th of May, when at anchor in Bearhaven, Bantry Bay. And it is equally painful for me to feel myself reduced to the necessity of calling on you to support me in my authority; but so deep-rooted are the evils that arise from a relaxed discipline, that without examples of the most serious nature, it is to be apprehended the services of this particular ship can no longer be made useful to the Country, or at all depended on by her commander.
>
>   It appears by various evidence that a plot has existed in the ship since soon after leaving Cawsand Bay, for turning the captain and such other officers as were obnoxious to the people out of her, and under pretence of grievances which are called insupportable; and for the execution of this intention various times have been proposed and rejected.
>
>   It was at last fixed, and perhaps accelerated, by the signal being made for the fleet to unmoor in Bantry Bay; when the conduct of the ship's company became marked with the

most unexpected acts of open and daring mutiny; the leading features of which I beg to relate; reserving the more minute points to appear on evidence, when you shall think proper to direct a trial of the respective persons whom I shall charge as principals therein.

At noon on Thursday, the 30th of May, I had left orders with the officer of the watch to call all hands at the usual time and direct one watch to clear the hawse, the other two to wash decks; and had gone into my cabin to dress. In this unsuspecting situation, the officer of the watch reported the ship's company aft with a complaint. Hearing a great noise I instantly ran out, and on my appearance the noise was much increased, the people, about two or three hundred, all pressing aft and crying out 'One and all, one and all: a boat, a boat'. I asked what the matter was, and was answered by Samuel Sydney, and Thomas Harrop and others, who were foremost in complaining of hard usage, flogging, etc., and muttered something about a letter to Lord Bridport which I repeatedly and vehemently asked for, saying on my honour I would carry it myself, or send an officer with it. To all this there was a constant cry of 'No-no-no-! a boat of our own! – a boat of our own!', and the more I endeavoured to pacify them and bring them to reason, the louder the noise became; many saying – Sydney, Harrop – and Jones, particularly 'We will have a boat, we'll take one'. This convinced me they were determined to go the greatest lengths, and was more than either my patience or my duty permitted me to bear. I only answered 'You will, will you?' and flew into my cabin for my sword, determined to support the King's service and my own authority; and to kill Sydney and Harrop who were addressing me and appeared to be the leaders.

Happily, that became unnecessary; the people flew off the quarter-deck, the letter was found and brought to me, the ring-leaders were seized, and peace restored to the ship, the regular duty of which began again. It remains for me only to produce my charges and evidence against the prisoners, and to request you will be pleased to order a court-martial to assemble for trial ...

This ultimately took place and three of the ringleaders received the death penalty.

In its time, Falmouth Bay has been the centre for many glamorous occasions. The Royal Navy, as we have seen, provided a distinguished presence there, not always in circumstances that could be called glamorous, but outstanding, certainly. Nelson himself had dropped anchor there; and it was to Falmouth Bay that the frigate *Pickle* came in with the news of the victory of Trafalgar. Napoleon Buonaparte also was a visitor in the *Northumberland* which was now on its way taking him to St Helena and exile. I must also record that Sir Francis Drake, with a fleet of five ships and 164 men, was in port on the fifteenth day of November 1577 intending to sail to Alexandria.

But by far the most dramatic occasion was when, on one morning in August 1779, the inhabitants of Falmouth woke up to find the bay full of ships. They were very alarmed because they had never seen anything like it before. They had good reason, too, to be alarmed for this silent, mysterious fleet of sullen ships looked to be nothing else but hostile, and right they were, for the fleet was French; and we were at war with France. Seventy-six enemy sail were counted manned by 20,000 men. The strength of our naval force at the time was fortunately strong consisting of thirty-eight sail of the line, frigates and fire-ships. The intentions of the enemy were never discovered, for the ships left in as mysterious a fashion as when they arrived, and the bay reverted to normal.

The Government augmented its naval claim on the splendid nature of Falmouth Bay by making it the base for the Post Office Packet service. This was created in 1670, and consisted of long distance mail carriers of the Post office carrying mail to Lisbon, the West Indies and America. In 1705 five packets were sailing between Falmouth and the West Indies (ninety-six days round trip), the vessels being of 150 tons and manned by thirty men. Two years afterwards the same number of Packets were employed between Falmouth and Lisbon (fifteen days return); in 1755, five Packets were employed between Falmouth and New York (90 days).

All through the eighteenth century the links that bound Falmouth Bay to the Post Office service grew steadily stronger, and as the number of ships increased so did the local traders prosper. The demand for stores was incessant, most of which had to be provided locally (due to poor communication). The use of the packets as carriers of mail, and gold and silver bullion, was invaluable for merchants and Government alike. In addition nearly 3,000 passengers were carried annually; but it was a hazardous occupation for vessels and crews and passengers who were open to attacks by privateers and warships.

However, the public recognised in the captain and crew that they were men of the elite, rather in the same mould as we regard the commandos of today, a glamorous mould of men who lived dangerously and lived well. Though it would be out of place for me to dwell too long on the packets here, I would much like to give the reader a glimpse of the life-style of their captains; and I beg those of my readers who have already been introduced to this in my *Proud Seas and Cornwall's Past* to bear with us for a moment.

'There was no place in England in which one could see so much of the gaiety and elegance of life as in the little village of Flushing, within the spacious harbour of Falmouth.' So wrote James Silk Buckingham in his autobiography.

Officers with long square-tail coats with large buttons on pocket and sleeves; square-toed shoes with massive silver buckles, and cocked hats. The boats' crews, with blue jackets and trousers, and bright scarlet waistcoats, overlaid with gilt buttons. The streets sparkled with gold epaulets, gold laced hats and brilliant uniforms.

Often the packets would be berthed one at each side of the quay, either to be scrubbed or paid off. This was the time the whole village celebrated, forgetting the past, and with no regard to what might happen on their next voyage. These were brave people, for it must be remembered that many packet boats left port never to return. It is recorded that between eighty and ninety widows were counted at one point of

Flushing's history as belonging to members of the packet crews. A safe return, therefore, was welcomed with dinners, balls, etc., held in captains' houses (or on the deck of the packet), and every night dances were in full force in the long rooms attached to public houses.

Owing to the plentiful supplies of wines and spirits which were smuggled ashore at the end of each voyage, no-one considered drinking unbecoming but rather the mark of a gentleman. It was thought a mean measure of hospitality to allow a guest at a great house to leave in a sober state.

Unfortunately, as time went by, the discipline in the Service got more and more relaxed, and by 1793 this indiscipline spilled over into a state of demoralisation; officers and crew had by now become accustomed to malpractices, such as smuggling, and much else. Let us see a little more the opportunities the Captain had for improving his position by skullduggery.

The Post Office representative in Falmouth was called 'the Agent', and, as often happened, he and the Captain joined forces in ways and means to cheat the Post Office. For instance, if it had occurred to any captain that by sailing a few men short of his complement he could make an increased profit by saving their victualling allowance, the Agent would turn a blind eye. If the captain wished to stay on shore, and send his ship to sea under charge of one of the officers, the Agent would accept, and send forward to London a certificate that he was ill, without asking any questions either as to the nature of the illness or the qualifications of the person appointed to command the Packet, who was not infrequently a common seaman.

The official records of the period are full of caustic references to the situation. I take from a paper, in the *Royal Institution of Cornwall Journal* of 1892, by Arthur Norway, an extract from one of them at random:

The Postmaster-General cannot but lament when looking at the absentee list in time of war to see how many reasons the captains are constantly urging to stay at home and of how little use they must consider their own use at sea.

There are at this time twelve packets at sea, and no less than ten of the captains of them ashore.

In the year 1800, the capture of several West Indian packets in quick succession provoked very strong remonstrances from the merchants of London, and rumours began to be circulated of large profits made by the officers of the packets going 'out', of being captured and losing their ships. No specific charge seems to have been made against any individual, but it was freely asserted that the goods which old custom allowed to be carried on the packets by the crew, though the law forbade them, were often insured for the homeward as well as the outward passage before the ship left Falmouth. If, then, all the goods were sold in the West Indies, it would be possible for the crew to remit the purchase money by a subsequent packet, or even by an armed merchant vessel, and to surrender themselves quietly to the first privateer they met.

They ran the risk of serving some years in a French prison, but on the other hand there was a good chance that the privateer would put them on shore in their own boat rather than accept the burden of keeping them on board as prisoners. Once they had reached England again they were secure from detection. Nobody would contradict them when they affirmed that the privateer had taken away large quantities of goods which they had not succeeded in selling. Their own assertion was the only evidence of what had occurred which it was possible to procure, and there was thus no difficulty in obtaining the full value of the insurance upon goods of which the purchase money was already in their pockets. That was the charge against the Falmouth captains, one involving so much base dishonesty that it was natural to hesitate before accepting it.

As soon as it reached the ears of the Postmaster General, an Inspector was ordered to proceed to Falmouth to look into it. The Inspector's report was to the effect that he believed it was not true. He gave no reason other than he was sure no insurance company would pay the value of the policy in the absence of an affidavit declaring precisely the quality and quantity of the goods on board at the time of capture. His report was adopted, but some doubt remained, it would seem, for they used the occasion to enforce a suggestion to the effect that Courts of Enquiry to investigate thoroughly the circumstances whenever a packet was captured.

At the end of 1799, an order was issued prohibiting private trade on the West Indian and American packets. Officers and crew were forbidden to carry goods of any kind upon their vessel in future.

It was not long before an infringement was uncovered when, in June 1801, two packets were captured on the Lisbon run. The packet *Earl Gower* was on her way home from Lisbon when she encountered the *Telegraphe*, privateer cutter, of fourteen guns and seventy men, a force considerably superior to her own. The captain, Deake, was undaunted, and made good use of his guns while endeavouring to escape, and might possibly have got clear off had not fully half his crew refused either to work the vessel or to fight her, and gone below in a body. Their action is scarcely comprehensible on any other ground than that they wished to be captured, through no fault of Captain Deake or his officers.

The second case is that of the *Duke of York* captured on 18 September 1803, while on her homeward voyage from Lisbon. The undisputed facts are these: The packet was chased throughout the day by a French pioneer of scarcely more than half her size, though more heavily manned. Towards evening, the master, who was acting commander at the time, consulted with the surgeon as to the proper course to take in view of the fact that the enemy was gaining on them. The surgeon advised surrender, and the master adopted his suggestion.

They came to this resolution while the enemy's vessel was still a mile distant from them; and before she had even fired a summoning gun they hauled down their colours. It was then seven o'clock and the night was falling rapidly. This circumstance, however, did not suggest to them the chance of escaping under the cover of darkness: it brought to their minds only the possibility that the enemy might not have seen their flag hauled down. To avoid any misapprehension on this subject, they sent a boat on board the privateer, and so, without attempting the slightest defence, they gave away their ship.

A Committee of Enquiry was held at Falmouth, but the captains who composed it put their questions in such a manner as to shield the culprits so far as possible, and finally satisfied themselves by finding that all the officers did everything possible to save their ship.

The Inspector of Packets thereupon set himself the task of investigating the matter. He traced, as best he could, the value of the goods which each sailor had on board, what insurances he had effected on the outward voyage and what on the homeward, and finally the sum he had gained by the capture. One man admitted that he had made £300. The surgeon, who had advised the surrender, had certainly gained £250, but by a remarkable lapse of memory he was quite unable to recollect what sum he had received from Lisbon for goods sold there, so that it was impossible to arrive at the full amount of his profit. The steward's mate was richer by £250, one of the seamen by £200, and most of the crew substantial sums.

The next step was to ascertain whether any of these men, and especially those who had made large profits on this occasion, had been captured before. The surgeon had been captured more frequently than any other man of the crew except three men. Three men had been captured three times, four other men four times.

After a long investigation the conclusion the Inspector came to was:

These papers prove beyond doubt that His Majesty's Packet could not have been captured if the skill and courage of her crew had been properly exerted. Their Lordships even incline to think that the French privateer might have been captured if our vessel had been carried into action with the spirit that characterises British seamen in general. No resistance was made. It was not even seen what the force of the privateer was. The packet was not even hailed or fired at by the enemy, and a boat was sent off to meet the privateer and to accelerate a surrender of which the seamen themselves speak as dishonourable and dishonest ... Under these circum-stances, my Lords, the Postmaster-General never will consent that ... the commander shall again be employed in the service, and the surgeon likewise ...

In the light of the facts, [concluded the report] the Inspector of Packets cannot help being of the opinion that if, during the war [with France], officers and seamen are permitted to carry out commissions on private transactions with merchandise, there is reason to fear that the loss of the packets on the Lisbon station may be very considerable, unless, indeed, under disinterested or high-spirited commanders.

In the light of these facts, it is very difficult to avoid the conclusion that some, at least, of the thirty-two packets captured between 1793 and 1815 had been given away in the same treacherous manner as the *Duke of York*. Of the thirty-two packets captured, twenty-one were taken on the *homeward* voyage.

It seems extraordinary such an elite organisation as the packet service should have had so large a skeleton in its cupboard; but though one may have the impression that the Government was responsible for its operation, it was not. The ships were owned by syndicates and carried gold and silver bullion and mails under contract to the Post Office.

Edward Bayntun Yescombe 1765-1803
It is by courtesy of Edward Yescombe, whose forbear was a Falmouth Packet commander at the end of the eighteenth century, that I am able to bring to you a fascinating account of the often bizarre life in the service of the Post Office, delivering mail overseas.

He was orphaned at an early age and was sent to sea as a midshipman at the age of eight years and eight months, later serving – many years later – as none other than one of Nelson's captains at the battle of Trafalgar, and being one of the pall bearers at Nelson's funeral.

In 1787 we find him being appointed Commander of the Packet boat *King George* and 'employed to carry mails to and from Falmouth and Lisbon.' Apart from mails, packets carried a few passengers and bullion, and other valuable goods, as can be imagined. There were four ships on the Lisbon station in Falmouth, and each round trip usually took two weeks each way. The aim was to provide a weekly service.

King George was a new ship of 200 tons, built in London in 1786: the investors putting up £4,000 as the original cost, and the Post Office giving this back over eighteen years, with 5% interest. As commander, Edward received about £18 per annum. However, as we have already learnt, it was notorious in Falmouth that packet ship crews supplemented their earnings by smuggling.

Captain Yescombe's grandfather was one of *the* Post-Generals, and his nephew took advantage of this in gaining favours from time to time; for example, an official minute of 1792 reads:

The Postmaster-General observes that two months' leave of absence every year to see a grandfather seems a very long period, and would be construed into a Precedent by the other Captains, which would give them a Claim to be absent equally long. The Postmaster-Generals therefore think that a month will be full time enough for Capt Yescombe to be absent, and that Sir Edward Bayntun will not expect him to ask for more.

In February, 1793, began the long war with France, which did not finally end until the defeat of Napoleon in 1815. As more and more of Europe was occupied by the French, the link which the Falmouth packets provided with neutral Lisbon became essentially vital. The ships were equipped with eight six-pound guns, and the crew was increased to 32 to help in defence of the vessel. However, the packets were no match for fully-armed French frigates or privateers, and they were instructed to sail fast and keep out of trouble.

But the war was not the only thing on Captain Yescombe's mind – in October 1793, he was given special leave of absence, and on 26 October he married Susannah Peters in the parish church of St Austell. Her father, Jonathan Peters, was vicar of St Clements, Truro. Like most of the packet captains they chose to live in Flushing. After the marriage celebrations were over, Captain Yescombe went back to sea.

On 13 July 1794, the *King George* left Lisbon for the voyage home, but a month later she had still not arrived. The British Consul in Lisbon 'entertained great apprehension for her safety, particularly as the wind had been for some days favourable for her, and it is said that several of the enemy's frigates were at sea'. News of her fate reached Falmouth on 14 August from the British frigate *Arethusa* which had met an American vessel at sea, from which it was learnt that the *King George* had been captured by a French frigate and taken into Brest. She had fallen in with the squadron of French frigates between Ushant and the Scilly Isles on 24 July. Several hours of evasive sailing were in vain, and Captain Yescombe was finally forced to surrender to the French 40-gun frigate, *L'Unité*, after having thrown the mails and official despatches overboard. Twenty-eight of the thirty-one crew on board, including Captain Yescombe, were taken on board *L'Unité* as well as five passengers. The French also carried over to their own ship fifty-nine bags of coin and a quantity of gold ingots, and several chests of silk and muslins – the latter, of course, were being smuggled.

The prisoners were then taken into Brest, where Captain Yescombe and two of his crew were interrogated by the local magistrate. In the record of interrogation – still preserved in Brest – Captain Yescombe is described as 'a tall man, dressed in a blue jacket, with gold buttons and braid and a cotton shirt and breeches'. He told the court that he was thirty years old, from Bath, in England, and that he had left Lisbon two weeks previously bound for Falmouth. This questioning was mainly aimed at getting strategic information, but the French did not have much success. A typical question was 'During your voyage, what ships did you meet? What countries were they from, and what route did they seem to be taking?' 'We saw a few small vessels at sea, but we did not get near enough to recognise them, and, in any case, as we were carrying despatches, we had strict orders not to deviate from our route.'

What were the contents of the papers you were carrying? I do not know, and even if I did know, I would not tell you! After this bold reply, the magistrate gave up.

The gold and the coin were confiscated, the muslins and silks sold by public auction, and the *King George* herself requisitioned into the French Navy.

After being held for some time in Brest, Captain Yescombe and his crew were transferred to the naval prison at Quimper. Many English sailors had been captured by this time, and conditions were very bad, with prisoners dying of hunger: and now a touch of romance appears when a lady related to the prison governor took pity on the Captain, and he was allowed to lodge at her house. In December 1794, according to his later story, she asked the prison official to hand back the paper she had signed taking responsibility for him, and six days later he escaped, making his way to Brest where he remained in hiding for several weeks. In due course, in January, 1795, he managed to get across the Channel to Plymouth in very poor health.

After being de-briefed, as we say nowadays, Captain Yescombe returned to Flushing, and by March had recovered sufficiently to claim that the £2,795 compensation paid out in his absence the previous November for the captured *King George* was insufficient because the valuation omitted, amongst other things, four brass compasses – £4 13s. 0d. – and thirty-two thimbles at 3d each.

Captain Yescombe never forgot what he and his crew went through in prison at Quimper, as this letter shows. He wrote it to the newly appointed Secretary of the Post Office, Francis Freeling, in March 1798.

Sir,

The Master, Surgeon, Petty Officers and Seamen of His Majesties Packet, *King George* if it meets with the approbation of their Lordships the Postmaster General (sic) request that you will have the goodness to subscribe for them at the bank, one month's pay towards carrying on the War. Most of the above people have felt in the prisons of Quimper how much the French hate the English and, particularly, English seamen. I am with the greatest respect etc. etc.

He sent with the letter a draft for £49, having previously subscribed £30 of his own money.

Captain Yescombe made arrangements to hire a temporary packet named the *George*, but he left this ship to be sailed by the Master, a Mr Bell. Although he had not broken any formal parole when he escaped, he was afraid that the French would treat him as if he had done so if they captured him again – and the penalty for breaking a parole was death: so the Captain of the vessel, Yescombe, stayed on shore while the *George* had some narrow escapes at sea which included fighting off a privateer off Finisterre, six of the crew being wounded, two seriously.

In the meantime a new *King George* was under construction in Plymouth and was finally delivered in October 1796. Captain Yescombe still remained on shore. The *King George* continued regular and, on the whole, uneventful voyages to and from Lisbon.

In June 1798, she was chased for a considerable time by the naval frigate *Cleopatra* who had mistaken her for a French ship. There were no signalling arrangements between the packets and Royal Navy, and this was a regular problem sometimes resulting in pitched battles before both ships realised they were on the same side.

In August 1798 the Post Office launched a lengthy investigation into the circumstances of Captain Yescombe's escape from France, and the reasons why he no longer went to sea. According to a report from Francis Freeling to the Postmasters-General, the Earl of Leicester and Lord Auckland, 'the propriety of the return of Captain Yescombe of the *King George* Lisbon Packet from France' had been questioned, and he had lately heard from Persons 'whom I thought were capable of giving me information, that the circumstances of his escape from the Country were extremely different from what they had been represented to me.'

Captain Yescombe's story was, however, accepted by the Post Office, but they then came to the conclusion that since he had not broken his parole there could be no reason to fear reprisals from the French should he be captured. In November 1798, Freeling wrote to Captain Yescombe formally ordering him to proceed to sea again 'because the Facts of your Escape from France have never been thoroughly understood until today – if they had been fully known no Argument could have arisen from it to have justified your absence even from a single voyage.'

'To the surprise and vexation' of Freeling, Captain Yescombe did not obey the order and wrote asking him to intercede with the Postmasters-General 'that I may not go to sea on worse terms than my Brother Officers as I am sure that were I again in the Power of the French they would treat me with all severity of a Person who had broke his Parole though I by no means did so.'

'It is impossible,' wrote the Earl of Leicester, 'to suffer such disobedience to our orders to pass unpunished.' A Court of Enquiry was convened in Falmouth, but in the end Yescombe was let off with a severe reprimand and a warning that if he still did not wish to go to sea he must give up command of his ship.

After three or four years of complying with this order, he became restless and doubtful about going to sea. The war was still on and by February 1803, he had been absent from his ship for five consecutive voyages, apparently with official approval, and wrote to Francis Freeling of 'calamitous events' to his family, asking for further leave. Freeling was now evidently on better terms with him since he described him as 'so excellent an Officer and so Worthy a Man' and leave for another voyage was granted. However, on 9 August 1803, the British Consul-General In Lisbon wrote as follows to the Foreign Secretary, London.

My Lord. It is with much concern that I have the Honour to inform your Lordship of the Capture of His Majesty's Packet, the *King George* – Captain Yescombe – which sailed from hence on the 22 July with despatches and a considerable quantity of specie on board. She was carried into Vigo from whence the accounts state that the Captain, and several of his Crew were badly wounded in the Engagement with a Privateer which took her ...

The *Auckland* Packet, which was probably carrying this despatch, met up at sea, 12 August, with a Swedish ship which turned out to be manned by the crew of the *King George*, who had chartered it in Vigo. Captain Yescombe had just died of his wounds.

In England, the news was received first from the French newspapers whose reports of the capture were reprinted in *Lloyds List* 23 August, and *The Times* the next day. The latter reported:

> She was taken by the *Reprisaille*, privateer, of Bordeaux, after an hour's contest, and having been boarded. The capture is the more to be regretted, as the Packet is known to have had jewels on board of considerable value, which were insured at Lloyds for a very large sum. It is said the jewels were thrown overboard, but this turned out to be incorrect, for a few days later the Cornish [sic] *Sherborne Mercury* reported from the French newspapers that they had found 15,000 carats of diamonds on board, estimated to be worth £45,000 together with 40,000 dollars.

When the Swedish galliot, crewed by the men of the *King George* arrived at the Scilly Isles, some six weeks after Captain Yescombe's death, his body was still on board – no doubt preserved in a barrel of rum, or something similar. There it was transferred to the Royal Navy *Providence* who carried it back to Falmouth Bay.

He was buried in the churchyard at Mylor: at the far side of the harbour the packet ships at anchor fired their guns as the funeral took place. The *Royal Cornwall Gazette* reported: 'All the captains of the packets in harbour attended, with most of their crews, and a vast concourse of people composed of nearly all the respectable inhabitants of Falmouth, Flushing, and the neighbourhood, to whom his memory will long be dear.'

Mignonette

We have seen now that the fair and lovely Falmouth Bay has been in intimate touch with occasions that have been of wide interest, to say the least. Now comes its way the relics of a hideous event that took place a hundred years ago five thousand miles away. 'Cannibalism at sea, the Mignonette Case' was the headline in the *Falmouth Packet* of 13 September 1884.

On 5 July there had sailed from Southampton for Australia the 19-ton *Mignonette*. She ran into a heavy storm when in the South Atlantic and suffered fatal damage when a massive wave disabled her and she sank – very swiftly. The crew of four had just time enough to get into the dinghy. Their predicament was fearful, for they had no provisions and they were hundreds of miles from land.

For twenty-four days Captain Dudley, mate Stephens, third hand Brooks and cabin boy Richard Parker drifted on the open sea. Obviously, they were in an acute state of privation. By the nineteenth day, Parker was dying, and the captain and mate decided to sacrifice one of the crew as their only chance – and Parker was the weakest, and he was the only one without dependants; so, praying for forgiveness, Dudley killed him, and the three remaining fed on his body for the next five days.

On the twenty-fourth day, having drifted 1,000 miles, they were spotted by the German barque *Montezuma*, and the three survivors were taken aboard together with the dinghy and its gruesome contents. Five weeks later, on 6 September 1884, the *Montezuma* sailed into Falmouth Bay, and within a week the town had become the subject of widespread notoriety, and the legal and emotional arguments for and against the *Mignonette*'s ill-fated crew raged throughout the land. The story they had to tell was certainly unusual. On their first night in the dinghy they had a shark to keep them company, very close. Then a more useful companion took its place, a turtle. This they killed and drank its blood. Fifteen terrible days followed, many of them with high seas. On the eighteenth day, they discussed the advisability of casting lots for one of them to be killed to provide food for the others. They had had no water for five days.

On the nineteenth day, and no sail appearing, it was decided to do this. Each man would take advantage of another asleep and make signs to the other as to who should kill Parker who lay in the bottom of the boat, his face hidden in the crook of his arm, lying still from utter exhaustion. They decided that the captain and the mate would do it together, and so it was that the wretched lad died. Captain Dudley made the most of it by running a small knife into the jugular vein, and catching the gushing blood in a tin. He divided it between them. They took off the boy's clothes and cut out his liver and his heart and these they devoured while still hot from the body.

On the following day, a little rain fell, and for the next four days they lived on young Parker's flesh. On the twenty-fourth day help came at last in the shape of the German ship *Montezuma*. The sailors were faced with hauling aboard the putrid and mangled remains of the boy which, after Captain Dudley had confessed to the German captain the reason, were thrown overboard.

On arrival in Falmouth the three survivors were taken to the Sailors' Home where Mr Cheeseman, the Receiver of Wrecks, received their deposition at the Customs House. They were taken to the borough prison and brought before the magistrates the following day. The charge was 'Wilfully, Feloniously, and with Malice aforethought, killing Richard Parker on the high seas.' Bail was asked for but refused. Later this was granted, a decision which was greeted in the court with applause.

Five of the highest legal functionaries of the realm assembled as a Divisional Court, and their dictum was that the killing of a fellow-creature by the survivors of a shipwreck on the high seas, even with the view of sustaining the lives of the remainder under the most terrible privations, is still, in the eyes of the law, murder. By the judge's direction the jury returned an especial verdict, and the Lord Chief Justice, at this trial at Exeter Assizes, did not put on the Black Cap, though the verdict was guilty. The prisoners were later sentenced to six months' hard labour.

Trefusis

Dominating one side of the Carrick Roads in Falmouth harbour, facing out toward Black Rock and the Bay is the solid bulky promontory of Trefusis. It was around its rocky feet that the *Queen* transport, in 1814, was wrecked. She had on board the troops returning from action in Spain in the Peninsular War, and 200 of them were lost.

At the top of this promontory, and still there today, is the Trefusis family mansion, and in a moment we are going to have a look inside, or I should say, we are going to eavesdrop as the squire shows a Mr Beckford round. Here we go: the date is 8 March 1787; and this is how Mr Beckford recorded the experience. He was, by the way, on his way to Portugal:

In this house dwelleth an ancient gentleman called Trefusis – what a lovely morning! how glassy the sea! How busy the fishing boats, and how fast asleep the wind in its old quarter! Towards evening, however, the wind freshened, and I took a toss in a boat with Mr Trefusis, whose territories exist halfway round the bay. His green 'hanging-downs' spotted with sheep and intersected by rocky gullies shaded by tall oaks and ashes from a romantic prospect in the style of Mount Edgcumbe.

We drank tea at the capital of these dominions, an antiquated mansion which is placed in the hollow of the summit of a lofty hill, and contains many ruinous halls and never-ending passages. They cannot be said, though, that they lead to nothing, for Mrs Trefusis arrived and terminated the prospect. She is a native of Lausanne. We should have very much enjoyed her conversation, but the moment the tea was over, he could not resist leading us around his improvements in stable, kennel, and ox-stall, although by now it was near pitch-dark, and we were obliged to be escorted by grooms and groomlings, with candles and lanthorns, a very necessary precaution because the wind blew no more violently without the house than within.

At dinner we had on the table a savoury pig and some of the finest poultry I ever tasted; and round the table two or three brace of odd Cornish gentlefolk, not deficient in humour or originality. About eight in the evening, six game-cocks were ushered into the eating rooms by two limber lads in scarlet jackets and after a flourish of crowing, noble birds set to with surprising keenness. Tufts of brilliant feathers soon flew about the apartment, but the carpet was not stained with the blood of the combatants, for to do

Trefusis justice, he has a generous heart and takes no pleasure in cruelty. The cocks were unarmed, had their spurs cut short, and may live to fight fifty such harmless battles.

IX

Mount's Bay

Hark to this splendid verse inspired by the Mount, in Mount's Bay – St Michael's Mount – two hundred years ago:

> Majestic Michael rises, he whose brow
> Is crown'd with Castles, and whose rocky sides
> Are clad with dusky ivy; he whose base,
> Bent by the storms of ages, stands unmoved
> Amidst the wreck of things – the change of time.
> That base encircled by the azure waves,
> Was once with verdure clad; the towering oaks
> Whose awful shades among the Druids strayed,
> To cut the hallow'd Mistletoe, and hold
> High converse with their Gods.

Half a mile or so from this grand and imposing castle on St Michael's Mount is the site of a small building which also has found a place in Cornish history, but that is the only thing the two have in common; for the little house the other side of Cudden Point earned its place in history by being the base of a notably successful smuggling family, the Carters of Prussia Cove in Mount's Bay.

Harry Carter was born in 1749 and died in 1809. His diary was found by one of his family, and from it we get a fascinating first hand account of a very individual lifestyle in the role of smugglers, born, so to speak of the respectable environment of Mount's Bay. The action takes place at the end of the eighteenth century and beginning of the nineteenth.

The autobiography was edited by John Cornish, and

published in 1894. I am glad to be able to offer to my readers more highlights from this authentic record by a spectacular, yet God-fearing law-breaker in what was then a glamorous calling. So, let us greet Harry and see what he has to say; but first, read the introduction by John Cornish who will set the scene for us:

The part of Cornwall to which the biography relates is the district lying between the two small towns of Marazion and Helston, a distance of about ten miles on the north-eastern shores of Mount's Bay. The bay is divided into two parts by Cudden Point, a small, sharp headland about two miles east of the Mount. The western part runs into the land in a roughly semi-circular shape, and is so well sheltered that it has almost the appearance of a lake, and, in fact, the extreme north-western corner is called Gwavas Lake.

From the hills that surround it the land slopes gently to the sea, and is thickly inhabited. The towns of Penzance and Marazion, and the important fishing villages of Newlyn and Mousehole occupy a large portion of the shore, and around them are woody valleys and cultivated fields. To the eastward of Cudden is in marked contrast. There, steep and rocky cliffs are only broken by two long stretches of beach, Praa Sand and Loe Bar, on which the great seas which come from the Atlantic have had a habit of hurling an embayed vessel on to the mounds of sand and shingle. A fine naval frigate, the *Anson*, was one of them, the *St Anthon*, a Portuguese treasure ship, another.

We will leave John Cornish for a moment to elaborate on the story of the *St Anthon*. In 1597, the *St Anthon*, belonging to King John III of Portugal, was sailing from Flanders, laden with a valuable cargo of silver, copper, jewels and cloth, when she was wrecked at Gunwalloe with the loss of nearly half her crew. The survivors subsequently accused some prominent local gentry of robbery with violence: two Commissions enquired, and the case went to the Court of Star Chamber. These defendants were William Godolphin JP, Thomas St Aubyn JP, John Milleton, Captain of St Michael's Mount JP, James Chynoweth of

Marazion Gentleman, Peter Treneves Yeoman, servant to Godolphin.

The contemporary MSS giving the fullest account of the wreck are the Petition to Henry VIII from Francisco Pessoa, an agent of John III, and the defendants' Answer to Star Chamber.

At the time of the wreck Portugal was a strong maritime power, and at Antwerp where she had a well-organized 'Factory', or trading organisation, her fleets exchanged the products of her discoveries in Africa, South America and the East for the metals and manufactured goods of Europe. England and Portugal had been allies since the Treaty of Windsor (1386) which stated that any robberies committed were to be the King's responsibility (and must be remedied within six months) and relations between the two countries were excellent.

Western Cornwall was far from the seat of government, difficult to rule, litigious and prone to rebellion. The generation before had risen for Perkin Warbeck, the Pretender to the House of York, and the generation to come were to rise for the new prayer book. As Carew noted in his Survey, there were no resident nobility there ('the King hath there no cousins'): and the gentry, closely related by marriage (all Cornishmen are cousins), were looked on by the people as 'Roytelets because they know no greater'.

Wrecks were regarded as manifestations of God's grace and as a hereditary right, and the customs regarding rights to wreck [cargo and vessel] were well established and strictly enforced.

In examining the events which followed the loss of the *St Anthon*, it is useful to bear in mind the subject of Tudor morality. This was such that the ethics of the age were not those approved today, and it is unfair to judge the actors too rigidly by our standards. A man esteemed worthy in Tudor times could do things that would exclude him from worthiness now. He could rob his neighbours by legal chicanery, take bribes in the performance of public duties, fawn and flatter with complete insincerity, burn his fellows for rejecting a creed, and hang them for necessity of State. Such things the State allowed, and before its last half-century there are few figures against whom some of these charges cannot be brought.

When considering the allegations of violence made by the Portuguese it should be remembered that in order to bring a case to the Court of the Star Chamber it was necessary for violence to be alleged, and in *some* Star Chamber cases these allegations were unfounded and were only made so that the dispute could be considered by the Court.

The *St Anthon* was the flagship under the command of Antonio Pacheco who was sailing in her with a crew of eighty-six. She was described as being a fine ship capable of tackling the usual bad weather of the Channel, but not the tremendous gale of 19 January when the ship

> by reason of the great and urgent tempest of winds and weather, and by the great outrages of sea at the time chancing at Gunwalloe in the county of Cornwall, was perished and drowned in the sea there, and divers mariners and other persons then being within the same ship were there also then piteously perished and drowned. [The ship was wrecked at a place called Porth Lingey, where the cargo was salvaged from a depth of one fathom. Porth Lingey is probably the cove now called Halzaphron, near Hingey farm.]
>
> By great difficulty and danger to life forty-five of the persons which also were then in the ship then escaped and were saved and came to land at Gunwalloe about eight of the clock in the forenoon of the same day. Which persons so saved with divers others of the King's subjects being inhabiting near thereabout, with great pain, labour and difficulty all that day and the next night and the morrow next following, endeavoured themselves to have saved and gotten out of the sea the goods to the use of the owners thereof – during which time divers and many of those persons which so laboured about, and for the saving of the premises were thereby put in great jeopardy and danger of their lives, and one of them being inhabitant of the county of Cornwall, then and there was piteously drowned, and perished.

Thus far in the story there is no conflict in evidence; but the evidence that followed the recovery of the cargo is the subject of two quite different accounts. According to the Portuguese:

> The Portuguese that came alive to land with help of the good men of the country saved the Saturday afternoon as much goods as did amount to a thousand ducats [£470] and above, and so the good people of the country, after the goods so saved by them, brought the goods to the Portuguese, and the Portuguese also brought the goods even as the men of the country brought the goods, and did well reward and recompense them for their labours and pains taken, and so they continued in saving until night.
>
> The said night thither came one John Wylliam, miller and servant to Godolphin, and two servants of Milleton, one of them being Trehanneck and the other named Geyge, an Irishman, with their swords drawn and their bucklers [shields] in their hands, came upon the Portuguese so being and saving of their master's goods. The above-named three persons, with many others in their company being their fellows took and spoiled from the Portuguese in their masters' names what it pleased them.
>
> On the morrow, being Sunday, there came to the Portuguese Chynoweth and in his company one James Beauchamp that could speak the language of Portugal and required and inveigled the Portuguese to make sale of the ship, the goods and merchandise. The Portuguese answered and said that 'The ship and goods were all only the King of Portugal's and so it doth appear upon our charter party whereof here is no man left alive that hath power to make sale thereof'. Then the Portuguese made their complaint unto Chynoweth how they were robbed and spoiled on the night past, and desired of him counsel. Then Chynoweth said 'if that one or two of you will go with me unto certain gentlemen being Justices of the Peace I think that they will cause you to have restitution of your goods again'. The Portuguese, being glad to be restored of their goods, sent with Chynoweth one of their fellows named Alvarez, and Chynoweth brought him to St Aubyn, Godolphin and Milleton, and then and there Alvarez made a complaint to

them of their robbing and spoiling of the night past. And then they answered and said, 'There is no remedy therein, for it is the custom of this country, and if you and your fellows will sell us the ship and goods we shall give you well, and, furthermore, we will do the best for you that lies in our power to make sale thereof'.

Then Alvarez answered that 'he, nor none other being there present had power to make sale thereof, for it is all only the King of Portugal's, and he who was his factor in this ship, in whose name the charter party was made, is drowned. And so Alvarez departed and went to his company whereat the Portuguese were lodged.

The said Sunday night there came to one Chenal's house, whereat the Portuguese was lodged, being near to the Strand whereat the ship was lost, one Richard Borno, servant to Godolphin, and John Polgrene, servant to John Vivian, with many of their fellows, with other servants of St Aubyn and Milleton with their weapons drawn broke into the house of the Portuguese and putting them in great fear of their lives, spoiled and took from them as much as they could carry away.

On the morrow being Monday, the defendants came nigh to the place whereat the ship was lost, and they sent to speak to Alvarez apart from his company, and advised him to make sale of the ship and goods unto them. Then Alvarez considered the great danger he and his fellows were in the two nights past and there was no remedy otherwise to do and for avoiding of further inconveniences, and as he made report to the King, his master, for safeguard of his life and his fellows, made sale of the ship, goods and merchandises as well of them that were in their custody and keeping to the value of 1,000 ducats.

After the bargain and sale made by Alvarez unto the defendants they would not suffer him to come no more among his fellows, but had him home into their houses, and used him at their pleasure. Oft times they took him behind them on their horses and rode about in the country among the King's subjects there inhabiting; and in the name of the King of Portugal took and spoiled from them as well as the goods that the Portuguese did give and deliver to them for the helping and the saving of the goods as otherwise.

Within a certain space after the defendants made as open unto the Master of the ship, and to all the residue of the Portuguese at Treneves' house at the town of Helston, and then caused Alvarez (with their power of servants), to come in upon the Portuguese, they being as merry as men ought to be at meat, and there and then took and spoiled from the Master and the residue of his company, all that they then had excepting their apparel. And as the Master and his fellows made report unto the King of Portugal they took as much plate, jewels and ready money as did amount to above a thousand Mark (£670).

And so Alvarez, Treneves and their servants departed from the Master and the Portuguese being then in great trouble and heaviness at being spoiled of all that they then had. Alvarez, with Treneves and the gentlemen's servants, brought and made delivery of all, the plate, jewels and ready money that they had taken from the Master and his fellows, unto St Aubyn, Godolphin and Chynoweth, and then they, seeing the great substance that they had there, were not contented that they had taken from the Master a bowl piece of silver, his chain and whistle, wherefore they made restitution, and sent unto the Master his bowl piece, his chain and whistle again. And so they retain and keep all the residue of the plate and jewels.

The defendants' version of the events that followed the landing of survivors is quite different. According to them, whilst the goods were being rescued:

Divers of the persons and mariners that were saved, perceiving their great misfortune to the intent to have somewhat for their relief and comfort, then and there craftily embezzled and conveyed divers parcels of goods so saved insomuch Alvarez, then being chief ruler, governor and curator of the goods, could have no certain knowledge where they had conveyed the same goods. Thus, avoiding more loss that in such form might ensue, Alvarez with other of the same person so saved, caused Godolphin and Milleton, who dwelt not past four miles from Gunwalloe, to be sent to have their aid and assistance for the obtaining, and saving, of the premises. And so Godolphin and Milleton came to them at Gunwalloe.

I think, by now, we have had enough of the arguments and counter arguments between the opposing claimants of the luckless *St Anthon*, and her cargo, and I will spare the reader any further effort in coming to a decision. But before we do leave the scene, before we glance for the last time at the now crumpled hulk of a fine ship on the beach of Mount's Bay, there is one matter to which one must in justice to the Portuguese refer.

It is a reminder that this event took place in 1527, a period in our history when standards of moral behaviour were much coarser than they are today. Then, a man could use violence in argument and be admired for it. He saw nothing wrong in accepting bribes for his public duties, and he could be hanged for an alleged offence against the State.

*

We stay in Mount's Bay, but I will bring my reader forward again to the nineteenth century, to the time when Harry Carter, smuggler, was active there, and return to John Cornish's description of the place.

With the exception of the little fishing station of Porthleven, there is not a place anywhere along the coast, from Cudden Point to the Lizard, large enough to be called a village. Inland, the country is in keeping with the coastline. Trees are very scarce, and the stone hedges, so characteristic of all the wild parts of West Cornwall, the patches of moorland, and the scattered cottages, make the whole appearance bare and exposed. Prussia Cove, around which much of the interest of the narrative centres, lies a little to the eastward of Cudden Point. There are really two coves divided from one another by a point and a small island called the Enez. The western cove, generally called 'Bessie's Cove', is a most

John Cornish (continued):

sheltered and secluded place. It is so well hidden from the land that it is impossible to see what boats are lying in the little harbour until one comes down to the very edge of the cliff. The eastern side of the point where there is another small harbour called 'the King's Cove', is more open, but the whole place is thoroughly out of this world.

The high road from Helston, through Marazion to Penzance passes about a mile from the sea, but at the time of which Harry Carter was writing, this district must have been unknown and almost inaccessible. The mother of Humphry Davy (born at Penzance, 1778) has left us a record that when she was a girl 'West Cornwall' was without roads, and there was only one cart in the town of Penzance, and pack horses were in use in all the country districts. This is confirmed by a writer in the *Gentlemen's Magazine*, who says that there were no roads in this district, the ways that served their purpose were merely bridle paths 'remaining just as the deluge left them and dangerous to travel over.

The main interest in Harry Carter's story is that it gives us an authentic picture of the climate for the smuggling which was carried on in the neighbourhood in the latter part of the 18th century and early 19th. Cornwall had long enjoyed a reputation for pre-eminence in this particular form of unlawful trade, and apparently not without some reason. There is evidence of this in letter written by George Borlaise, who was agent to a Lieutenant General Onslow, complaining of the fact that smugglers were everywhere; 'smugglers, the coasts here swarm with smugglers', and asking that soldiers might be stationed in the district. [This correspondence (the Lanisley letters) is of great interest, see Appendix B.]

That smuggling prevailed to the degree that it did is not to be wondered at, for the law must have had a very small hold on such a rough and scattered population, living so far away from any of the large centres of England, and in such a narrow county, too. No one lived far from the sea so the miners took to smuggling as readily as the fishermen, a trip to Roscoff or Guernsey being a pleasant change after a spell

John Cornish (continued):

underground or working the stamps, or crushing the ore.

These tinners were a rough, reckless lot, and if riots and bloodshed were more scarce in West Cornwall than in some parts, it must have been due to the judicious absence of the Customs officials rather than any qualities in the smugglers. The smuggling was so universal that every fishing village and cove had its own story that blended later into legend; every cavern is assumed to have been a smugglers' cave so far as the holiday visitor is concerned (sic).

Prussia Cove, beyond all others, has the richest store of history. Here are little harbours cut out of solid rock which still are occupied, sometimes, by fishing boats. One can see a roadway partly cut and partly worn, crossing the rocks below high water mark, and caves of which the mouths have been built up which are reputed to be connected with the house on the cliff above by secret passages. The house referred to was burnt down early in this century, the house that is there now being of a later date.

In the legends of the Cove the personality of John Carter, (Harry's elder brother) looms so large that his associates are almost, if not entirely, forgotten, and everything centres around him; and Harry who is the diarist. It was John who cut the harbours and the road, it was he who adapted the caves. He is the 'hero' of most of the tales which are told of the good old days. One of these stories is worth recording here. On one occasion, during his absence from home, the excise officers from Penzance came around in their boats and took a cargo of his which had lately arrived from France. They took it to Penzance where it was secured in the Custom House store. In due course, John Carter returned to the Cove and learnt the news. What was he to do? He explained to his comrades that he had agreed to deliver the cargo by a certain day, and his reputation, as an honest man, was at stake. He must keep his word. That night, a number of armed men broke open the store at Penzance and John, the 'King of Prussia', took his own again, returning to the cove without being discovered.

In the morning the officers found that the place had been

John Cornish (continued):

broken into during the night. They examined the contents, and when they noted what particular things had gone, they said to one another that John Carter had been there, and they knew it because he was an honest man who would not take anything that did not belong to him: and John Carter kept his word to his customers.

It was characteristic of the history of smugglers everywhere that they enjoyed the support of popular sympathy. This was certainly the case in West Cornwall where the farmers, the merchants and, it was rumoured, the magistrates, used to find the money with which the business was carried on, investing small sums on each voyage to Guernsey or Brittany. Harry Carter, finding shelter at Marazion when the Government was offering a reward for his capture, was helped by an unnamed influential man of the neighbourhood: and it is difficult to avoid the conclusion that there must have been some powerful influence exerted in his favour to obtain his exchange from prison in France in 1778 during the war with France. And what can we make of his commission to go privateering against the Americans during the American Civil War? The Government had then passed a measure to encourage privateering by authorising the Admiralty to grant commissions: apparently English seamen everywhere were readily taking advantage of the opportunities so offered for their enterprise.

However, to obtain such a commission the applicant had to find securities of whose 'sufficiency' the commissioners had to satisfy themselves. The applicant also had to send full details, of course, of the ship, specifying the number of guns and other potent matters. Surely, Harry Carter could not have ventured to place himself in the hands of the Government in this way without a friend at Court. It certainly seems a fair inference to make, from their popularity and fame, and from the fact that the two brothers rose to leading positions amongst the smugglers while still comparatively young.

The accounts of the actual smuggling in the pages of the

John Cornish (continued):

diary are not very detailed because at the time that Harry Carter was writing (1809) John Carter and the 'Cove boys' were still at it, and Prussia Cove (Porth Leah is its true name) had not yet ceased to be a centre for the smuggling fraternity. This would also explain the absence of particular reference to any of his companions. This reticence that we have to accept is quite compensated for by the variety of his later experiences; for example, to have been a prisoner in France during the Reign of Terror, and at a time that the Convention had decreed that no quarter should be given to an Englishman [Carlyle, *French Revolution*, vol III], that is in itself no small claim on our attention.

It would seem that the English who were, of course, prisoners of war, were placed on the same footing as the 'aristocrats' and 'suspects', of whom there were so many as prisoners that it was necessary to utilise convents, and even private houses as prisons.

A French writer of the time, Alexandrine des Echerolles, describes in her book *Private Life in Public Calamities* life under such unusual circumstances. Bread was distributed daily to the prisoners, and their pitchers filled every morning with fresh water. Those who could not pay the turnkeys for their trouble evidently got very little, so the rich used to bestow alms upon the poor in this form. Once a fortnight they were supplied with fresh straw or what was called such, each person receiving an armful. She mentions that, by degrees, the prisoners managed to make themselves more comfortable by introducing tables and chairs, and mattresses which they were compelled to leave on their removal to other prisons. This coincides with Harry Carter's account, and he seems to have shared their anxiety as to the fate of his friends and the common anticipation of the guillotine.

From the very first lines of his biography, Harry, the successful smuggler, is shown to be a deeply sincere God-fearing Christian. In no part of England did the teaching and influence of John Wesley obtain such a hold as in Cornwall. At the time of his first visit Wesley speaks of the natives of this distant country as 'those who neither feared God nor regarded man' (Wesley's Diary, 17 May 1743): he accuses the Cornish of wrecking and murdering those who were washed ashore; and describes their pastimes as 'hurling, at which limbs were often broken, fighting, drinking and all other manner of wickedness.'

And now we come to the Autobiography of Harry Carter, a Cornish smuggler:

I was born in the year 1749 in Pengersick in the parish of Breage, in the County of Cornwall. My mother had ten children, eight sons and two daughters, eight of whom lived to maturity. My father was a miner who was a hard labouring man, and brought up his family in what we called decent poverty. My oldest and younger brothers were brought up to good country scholars, but the rest of my brothers with myself, as soon as we was able, was obliged to work in order to contribute a little help to support a large family, so that I never was kept to school, but only to read in what we called then the great Book.

As for our Religion we were brought up like the rest of our neighbours, to say some prayers after we were in bed, and to go to Church on particular times as occasion served us.

When I was about 8 or 9 years old, my brother Francis was about four years older than me. He joined the Methodist society in Rudgeon, soon after found peace with God, and as him and me were most times sleeping and waking together, he revealed himself unto me and told me the place and time that he received the Comeforter, I, seeing such very great change in him, as before time, he was a very active boy, I firmly believed the report. From that time I firmly believed that unless I was born again I should in no case see the kingdom of God, so that convictions followed me sharp and often, sometimes me constrained to weep bitterly. But alas! As I grew up they went fewer and fainter.

Aboute 9 or 10 years old I worked at the mine at the stamps, and continued till I was about 15. I worked there until aboute 17 and from thence went with my two elder brothers to Porth Leah, or the King's Cove, afishing and smuggling, and at times (when 18 or 19) with people from Folkestone, and sometimes with the Irish, as super cargo whom we freighted.

When I was aboute 25 I went in a small sloep, about 16 or 18 tons, with two men besides myself, a smuggling where I had very great success, and after a while I had a new sloop built for me, about 32 tons. My success was rather beyond common, and after a time we bought a small cutter of aboute 50 tons and aboute 10 men. I sailed in her one year, and I suppose I made in her more safe voyages than have ever been made since.

So by this time I began to think something of myself, convictions still following sharply at times.

I allwayse had a dislike for swearing, and made a law on board if any of the sailers should swear he was punished. Nevertheless, my intention was not pure. I wanted to be noted to be something out of the common way of others. Well then, I think I was counted what the world would think a good sort of man, good-humoured, not proude etc.

But man is short-sighted, deceitful and desperately wicked, oftentimes burning and boiling within in a blaze of passion, though not to be seen without. Nevertheless, in the meantime was capable to be guilty of outward sins the same as others of my companions, and often times, when out on a party, crying and praying to keep me from a particular sin, was often the first that was guilty of committing it. Then consciense, after staring me in the face, oh what a torment I would feel! So I went on sinning and repenting for many years sinning and repenting.

In 1977, we built another cutter, about 197 tons*, expecting to make all our fortunes in a hurry:

---

* The sizes of all vessels are given in old measurement. Before 1835 the sizes of all vessels were fixed by an excruciatingly elaborate rule. This is how it goes: Subtract three-fifths of the greatest breadth from the length of the keel, multiply this by the breadth, and the result by half the breadth; divide the result so obtained by 94, and the answer is the size of the ship in tons. Harry Carter's new cutter of 197 tons, in modern measurement, would be about 120 tons.

Well, that was not to be. Harry Carter was at sea with her in December of that year about Christmas time and had cause to go to Guernsey to pick up cargo for the next 'run', and to have a repair to his bowsprit, but on his arrival he was advised to go to St Mâlo. However, for want of Custom house papers he was seized upon by the French Admiralty office at St Malo who unbent his sails, took them on shore, and confined Harry and the crew to be on board, with a guard of soldiers, as prisoners, allowing never more than two men on deck at a time. No boat was permitted to come alongside, no letters to be sent or received.

However, Harry had a way with him, and it was not long before his genius for gently getting his way yielded results:

I soon got the favour of the officer in command, and I could send letters on shore. I sent an express to Guernsey, likewise to Roscoff, when there was soon certificates come to show that I was not a pirate. They had some justification, I must say for thinking this, I having sixteen carriage guns on board and thirty-six men without any maritime pass, or anything to show for them. Notwithstanding, they certainly knew what I was.

I think it was on 30 January 1778, and I think the latter end of March, there came an embargo on all British bothams. [The treaty between France and the Americans was made on 6 February 1778.] They keept me on board with all the people until, I think, 1 May, when they took me on shore to examine me, and about four o'clock I was sent, with a strong guard unto the Castle. This was a strange sight to me, the first prison I ever saw the inside of, the hearing of so many iron doors opening and shutting. So I was put up in the top of that very high Castle, in a criminal jail, where there was a little dirty straw and no much else. So after looking round a little to see my new habitation, I asked of the jailer to send me a chair to sit on, and something to eat as I took nothing for the day; but as the jailor left me hearing the rattling of the doors and the noise of the keys, I began to reflect, where am I now? I shall shorely never come out of this place whilst the war lasts. Shorely, I shall die here.

I suppose, in the course of half an hour, I heard the keys as before for a long time before I saw any person, then in came a man with a chair, my bed, and a little soup etc. I sat myself down in the chair, looked at my dinner, but then began to weep bitterly. I had not only lost my liberty, but the cutter also, which was my God. My liberty was gone, my honour was gone, my property, my life, God, all was gone; and all the ten thousand pounds I expected to get privateering was gone, as there was a commission sent for me against the Americans before I left home.

There I walked the dismal place, bewailing my sad case. But in the space of about two hours, two or three of my people were sent to join me, and before night, I think about eighteen of us filling the small room. Then we began to sing and make a noise, so that some of my tears vanished away; hope of life sprung up, and as the French were such flatterers in general, a very little hope for the cutter. The remainder of the ship's company were put in the town criminal jail. We was all kept in prison until aboute the 20 or 21 day of the same month, when early in the morning were took out by strong gard of soldiers, sent to Dinan prison of war, where we then had plenty of room.

I suppose we were about six or seven of us that every evening joined to sing psalms in parts etc: but this would not satisfy me, I know there was no Religion in this at all, but one night as I was asleep, as we lay on the floor side by side, I dreamed that I heard like the voice of an angel saying unto me, 'Except thou reform your life, thou must totally be lost for ever'. There was something more that he said but I cannot now remember it.

When I awaked I was in a lake, sweat from head to foot, and all my body in a tremble. Nothing but fear and horror in my mind. Next day took great care to lett no person know anything of the matter. I think I was in prison five or six weeks until my oldest brother, John [John of Prussia Cove] was brought to join me, as he came to St Malo just after I was stopped, from Guernsey, with the certificates from the Governor in order to try and liberate the cutter and me. Well then, this almost as great a trial as any, he being the head of the family, and thought the business must come to an end at home. We was keept both in prison until, as I think, some time in August, and was sent on parole about forty miles in a town called Josselin. However, we was keept in different places in the country until the end of November in 1779, when we were private exchanged by the order of the Lords of the Admiralty, in the exchange of two French gentlemen sent to France, in our room. When we got back home to the Cove we found the family alive and well, but with the loss of the cutter, and the business not managed well at home, as my brother was then a prisoner, and away from home about two years, the family in a low state.

A big change of occupation now faced Harry. On 24 October 1788, now without a vessel of his own, he sailed as crew from Mount's Bay for Leghorn, Italy, in the ship, *George*, Capt Dewen, Master. He was accompanied by his brother John, and a boat from King's Cove was put on board, too. Spiritually speaking, he was in a bad way as he writes:

I think I was allmoste like a dead man; I thought little or nothing about my wife or child, or anything in this world, but was earnestly crying for mercy. I had a little cabin to myself to lodge in where there was only a single partition between me and the men. At first it was a great pain for me to hear them swearing, but after a little while I took no notice of it. I had sume very good books to read with me, but they were not of the Spirit of God. I remember sume times reading, when I could not understand becoming so peevish and fretful that I could heave the book overboard. Then what torment in my poor soul I felt. Then to think surely the mercy of God is clean gone from me. Oh, what a burden life was unto me. At them times I seldom prayed less than, in secret, twelve times a day and night, and when I could pray with a little liberty, I should be in hope of mercy, and at other times kneel down and groan without one word brought to my remembrance, then allmost ready to give up all, saying 'all my prayers is no use at all. God pays no respect unto them – but still I dare not give up praying. I would look back afterwards and see that I was all prayer.

Poor Harry, he really was in a sad way but, as was usually the case, his spiritual torment was not to last long, for faith is a wonderful friend, keeping us close to Christ who is never more than a thought away from anyone.

Some ten days or so after making Leghorn Captain Dewen got a freight to take to Barcelona where he was then to load with brandy to take to New York. Harry's reaction was that he was very glad to hear it as he had heard there were Methodists there and he hoped he would fall in with some of them to give him instruction. So it was to be. They sailed from Leghorn in January 1789, and arrived at New York the following April. The long journey was accomplished without any problem excepting his feeling of inadequacy in the eyes of God; and this provoked cries of despair such as:

> I remember on my passage one day, scudding before the wind, very cold weather, and a very big sea, looking back over the starn. I thought I should be very glad to be tyed with a rope and towed after the ship for a fortnight, if that would get me into the favour of God. But alas! I know all such works would not merit anything from God as salvation.

That mood was not to last long, for he was soon to make very many friends from among the Methodist community, very soon becoming a most appreciated preacher. And he soon got a job working for a farmer. Well, now with the rather lovable rogue, Harry Carter, having seemingly found contentment for a while in a far distant country, we will turn our attention to Mount's Bay again, bypassing the Carters' base at Prussia Cove, and devoting a little time to the lawful activities relating to St Michael's Mount.

I see in my mind the elegant little town of Penzance as the queen of the bay, and I style the Mount as her king, for the two of them together have drawn history to the bay, a varied history of violence and peace, of an aspect exciting the attention of monks and nuns and gentry, of people, strange people at that.

For example, in the summer of 1760, when the country was deeply in the Seven Years War, and not withstanding the splendid successes of 1759, the nation still felt the always threatening invasion by France of our shores. One night the people of Penzance were roused by the firing of guns, and soon after, by the intelligence of a large ship of strange appearance having run on shore on the beach towards Newlyn. Great numbers of persons crowded to the spot, where they were still more astonished and shocked by the sight of men still stranger than their vessel, each armed with a scimitar and with pistols. It was now obvious they were Moslems, and a vague fear of Turkish ferocity, of massacre and plunder, seized the unarmed inhabitants, just awakened from their sleep in the middle of the night.

A volunteer company obeyed, however, with alacrity the beat to arms, and 172 men were conducted, or driven, into a spacious building which then stood on the Western Green. Eight men were found to be drowned. Before morning it was ascertained from themselves, by some who understood *lingua franca* that the ship was an Algerian Corsair, carrying 24 guns, from six to nine pounders, and that the Captain had steered his vessel into Mount's Bay and run it against the shore thinking he was safe in the Atlantic ocean at about the latitude of Cadiz, thus committing an error of thirteen degrees of latitude.

The instant it was known the sailors were Algerines, a fear seized the town and neighbourhood, scarcely less formidable than the other of massacre and plunder – namely, of the plague. The Volunteers, however, kept watch and ward to prevent all intercourse.

Intelligence was conveyed to Plymouth, and orders were said to have been issued for troops to march from Plymouth for surrounding the whole district; but most fortunately the local authorities ascertained that no cause whatever existed for such a precaution, and the orders were countermanded.

When it was found safe to visit the strangers, curiosity attracted the whole neighbourhood. Their Asiatic dress, long beards and moustachios, with turbans, and the absence of all covering from their feet and legs, their dark complexion and harsh features of a piratical style, made them objects of terror and suspense.

They were, on the whole, treated kindly. Their vessel had totally disappeared, and consequently, after some delay, a ship of war took all the men on board and conveyed them back, all the way to Algiers.

*

There had been in the year 1595 another kind of visitation to the bay by a foreign armed force which, though consisting of only two galleons, caused much damage to property in Mousehole and Newlyn, and Penzance, too.

The Spanish Factor

The Spanish Armada, though very closely a national event, was related very much to the West Country in terms of who was responsible for England's victory. Drake, Raleigh, Hawkins? The defence was mainly provided by Plymouth so that the palm belongs wholly to Devon.

However, Cornwall had a share. Walter Raleigh was then 'General of Cornwall'. The blow might have fallen on West Penwith, as it did seven years later, in 1595. On 19 July 1588, the news arrived that the Armada had been seen off the Cornish coast. Perhaps already intelligence had got wind that Mount's Bay was the rendezvous selected.

The rest belongs to English, not Cornish, history. The story of the battle outside Plymouth Sound, the fireships off Calais, the storms in the North Sea, the wrecks on the Irish coast, is all well known: but not so well known, of course, but very dramatic, was the return of the Spaniards, those few years later, with an invading force on Cornish soil.

It was a misty July morning in 1595 when four foreign ships were seen approaching Mousehole. The little town lay in its usual tranquil peace, suspecting nothing untoward; it was unarmed and defenceless.

Boats were seen to be lowered on the foreign ships and they made for Point Spaniard to the west of the town. Here some two hundred Spanish soldiers landed, armed with pikes and muskets. They sent off sections to occupy and ravage the scattered farmsteads of Paul as far as Churchtown. The main body advanced on Mousehole. the fishermen were totally unprepared to meet in battle the trained troops of Alva and Parma, and they fled in terror. Squire Keigwin, alone, made a stand for his mansion [now the Keigwin Arms], and was killed.

The town was set on fire. Mousehole, excepting the Keigwin mansion, was reduced to ruins. The church at St Paul's fared no better. It was burnt likewise. Two pillars of the chancel alone mark what it once was.

That morning, Sir Francis Godolphin had intended going to Penzance, but he had seen the fire and smoke from the hills, and met the Mousehole fugitives at Penzance Green. He sent messengers at once to Sir Francis Drake and Sir John Hawkins, to Plymouth for help, and then collected together some 100 men with thirty or forty firearms of which many were unserviceable. These Cornishmen, however, clamoured to be led on against their foes, to stop them from further ravages.

This reaction led the Spaniards to re-embark and move their four galleys into Mount's Bay, anchoring just off Newlyn. Again, they landed troops, and they climbed the hill behind the town and formed in order of battle. They were now 400 strong, sending out skirmishers to the top of the hill. Seeing only Godolphin's little band, they advanced toward Penzance. Sir Francis, observing their move, retired into the town. As soon as the Cornishmen entered the Green, the artillery from the galleys opened fire. The cannonade was not so serious as alarming. Only one constable was unhorsed, but the untrained Cornishmen were much shaken by it. 'Some', says Carew in his *Survey*, 'fell flat on the ground, and others ran away.'

Sir Francis did not have much chance against those 400 warriors who Don Diego de Buchero was bringing against him; even so, he called on his men to make a stand at Penzance. In the panic that prevailed this was forgotten or, at least, fell on deaf ears. He found at the Market Place only two men who could be called resolute, and some ten or twelve others who followed him, most of them his own servants; the rest, frightened men, all fled.

The Spaniards entered Penzance in three parts, Sir Francis finding his position hopeless. The houses behind him were set on fire, and soon the town was, it seemed, in a mass of flames and so, also, was Newlyn.

Having made these innocent little towns a desolation, the Spanish troops re-embarked in their galleys.

As evening approached, the Cornish rallied, and with help from other parts, encamped on Marazion Green to defend the Mount and the road into the interior.

Next day, 24 July, the Spaniards made a reconnaissance on the west side of the bay, but seeing that the Cornish now appeared to be resolute, they re-embarked, moving their ships further off from the shore. On the third day (25 July 1595), the long desired help from Plymouth arrived. Sir Nicholas Clifford and Sir Henry Harris were in command of the troops while the English fleet was making for the Lizard; but they came too late. The wind veered from SE to NW; the Spaniards took advantage of it, and made off before the English Commanders could punish them for their audacity.

Thus ended the only important landing of the Spaniards as enemies on British soil.

A curious record of the Spanish landing is to be found in the Paul register. The record of the burning of the parish church, and the burial entry of three men killed by the enemy is there recorded, an entry that reads strange in the records of an English parish church.

And this ... this damaging, but minor invasion, is the last time any hostile troops have set foot on the United Kingdom. It was 400 years ago.

*

I would like to refer now to a minor invasion of a very different sort at the beginning of this century when the beauty of Mount's Bay was discovered by artists from both the United Kingdom and from abroad. The Newlyn Art Colony was created to take advantage of the wonderful quality of the light in this part of the world (St Ives has an art colony for the same reason).

Their pictures are held in great esteem in the art world and fetch large prices today. I would like to introduce you to Stanhope Forbes and hear how and why the colony took root, and how the 'foreigners' built a very close relationship with the fishermen of Mount's Bay. Let us hear from Stanhope Forbes's own reminiscences of Newlyn and its group of artists.

It would seem unnecessary to explain to any patriotic Cornishman the charm of his native county, to show wherein lies the fascination which it possesses for the artist; but the question is so often asked, What tie binds them to this district? that I will invite the questioner to ramble with me along the cliff and through the narrow streets of which Newlyn is composed, whilst I point out its features and tell the story of our connection with the place.

Let us meet on the little bridge at the entrance to the village, the bridge which I remember so well first crossing some fifteen years ago. I had come from France, where I had been studying, and wandering down into Cornwall, came one spring morning along that dusty road by which Newlyn is approached from Penzance. Little did I think that the cluster of grey-roofed houses which I saw before me against the hillside would be my home for so many years.

What lodestone of artistic metal the place contains I know not, but its effects were strongly felt, in the studios of Paris and Antwerp particularly, by a number of young English painters studying there, who just about then, by some common impulse, seemed drawn towards this corner of their native land.

It is difficult to say who was the original settler, for painters seem always to have known of the attractions of the place, Mount's Bay, and it is curious to think of the number of painters, many of whom have attained distinction, who visited this coast about then. There are plenty of names amongst them which are still, and I hope will long be, associated with Newlyn, and the beauty of this fair district, which charmed us from the first, has not lost its power and holds us still.

Here is the village before us, a busy little port, so different to that which I can remember when first it met my eye. In place of those two fine piers which now stretch out and form such an excellent harbour for the fishing fleet, only that little

Stanhope Forbes:

weather-beaten structure out yonder existed, capable at the most of giving shelter to a schooner or perhaps one or two fishing boats.

The brown-sailed luggers would in those days lie at their moorings out in the bay, or in rough weather seek the shelter of Penzance harbour. Yet though scarcely so large and important, the little port was active and picturesque, and the commerce of the place, carried on under more primitive conditions, was none the less attractive to an artist's eye.

From the first I was fascinated by those wet sands, with their groups of figures reflected on the shiny surface, which the auctioneer's bell would gather around him for the barter of his wares. If you look back now towards Penzance you will see, stretching out far into the bay, the sands at low tide. It was there that I elected to paint my first Newlyn picture, and out on that exposed beach, for many a month, struggled over a large canvas. I blush to recall what my models must have suffered posing for these early works of mine, and am only consoled by so often meeting healthy strapping lasses, or bronzed-faced young fishermen, whom I can remember as children shivering on the beach or roasting in the August sun whilst a young and over-zealous painter, forgetting all but his work, wrestled with the difficulties of light and shade.

It was part of our artistic creed to paint our pictures directly from Nature, and not merely to rely upon sketches and studies which we could afterwards amplify in the comfort of a studio. It is a debatable practice, and this is no place to argue such technicalities, but I mention it because, being strongly held by many of us, it imparted a noticeable feature to the village. Artists are common enough objects by the seaside; but it was scarcely so usual to see the painter not merely engaged upon a small sketch or panel, but with a large canvas securely fastened to some convenient boulder, absorbed in the very work with which he hoped to win fame in the ensuing spring; perhaps even the model posing in full view of the entire populace, the portrait being executed

Stanhope Forbes:

with a publicity calculated to unnerve even our practised brother artist of the pavement.

These singular goings on of the newcomers at first provoked much comment from the inhabitants, but by degrees they grew familiar with such strange doings, and scarce heeded the work which progressed before their eyes. Even the small folk grew tired of gazing, and at that dread moment when the school doors opened and let loose upon their chosen victims the arch tormentors of our race, a few moments of misery would ensue, and the harassed painter, with a sigh of relief, would find himself alone, once more free to continue his labours undisturbed.

Painters have an easy way of walking into other people's houses, calmly causing their occupants no little inconvenience. It is this habit of theirs which perhaps causes them to congregate in places where their oddities are known and their motives understood. When one considers the interest aroused by our proceedings, it speaks well for the good nature of the village folk that I can scarcely ever remember asking permission to set up my easel without it being freely accorded. With such favouring conditions it may be guessed that the place soon became a veritable artists' paradise, free from the drawbacks and hindrances that so commonly beset us.

Let us on through the village, glancing as we go at the harbour, with its busy life so full of interest, for the mackerel fishery is in full swing, and alongside the quay are moored the laden boats; looking down upon them is a motley crowd of fishermen and fishwives, salesmen and onlookers. Down that little lane formerly stood an old foundry, in which were cast or forged the capstans and other iron gear belonging to the fishing fleet, an interesting old place which has now unfortunately ceased to exist. Here, too, is the village post office, and around it those quaint old houses which served Walter Langley for the background of his dramatic picture 'Among the Missing', and which with many another picturesque corner will be preserved long after the progress of civilisation, as I suppose we must politely term the

Stanhope Forbes:

hideous invasion of the modern builder, has swept them away.

Following a narrow winding lane, we come down upon a beach which separates the two distinct villages of which Newlyn is composed – viz. Street-an-nowan and Newlyn town. This has always been a favourite haunt of the artists, and here we shall surely find one or two camped out, though not so many perhaps as in former years, for glass houses and studios have sprung up, and with advancing years we have grown bashful and shy of being overlooked. From here we obtain what is perhaps the most characteristic view of Newlyn. Alas! again many an old house, which made the irregular line along that uneven cliff still more interesting, has been pulled down and its place filled by some terribly commonplace modern structure, devoid of character and charm. However, let us be thankful that the new piers which we see so well from here are as thoroughly satisfactory to the eye as they are fitted for the work for which they were constructed. Severe and simple, they are yet pleasing to look upon, and have added to the beauty of the harbour rather than in any way marring it. At the end of one of them is a small lighthouse, which I can never contemplate without certain uneasy sensations. For off that pier head, day after day for months, I painted in a crazy old fishing boat, which lay at anchor there, and with unsteady hand endeavoured to dodge the motion of the waves.

Leaving the beach we ascend into Newlyn proper, and soon find ourselves in what might be termed the Melbury Road of this town. It boasts of the characteristic name of Trewarveth Street, which means, I believe, the street of the hill. Fortunately we are ascending, for it is a perilous journey to make one's way down its ill-paved surface.

That old thatched cottage, with a window in its roof, is scarcely a remarkable edifice, but Newlyn painters point to it with pride as the little studio in which Frank Bramley painted his 'Hopeless Dawn'. It stands at the corner of a little lane which some wag has christened the 'Rue des Beaux Arts,' a name which, painted in large letters on a board,

Stanhope Forbes:

serves to mystify the villagers greatly.

Just beyond here you can see a black gate, and alongside it a threatening notice warning parents that the direst penalties of the law await any unhappy urchin who strays within these portals. Be reassured: the Newlyn painters whose sanctuary this is are upon most excellent terms with the small fry of the village, and merely wish to have peace and quiet reigning round them when at work. Indeed, it is fortunate for us that the relations of the artist to the villagers have always been so cordial and satisfactory. Scores of the village folk, young and old, men, women and children, have sat to us and bear no malice – indeed, take pride in successes in which they rightly feel they have their part. And truly to the models is due no small amount of the success the place has had. What better material could artists have wished for? A fine-knit race of men and women, engaged in a healthy and picturesque occupation, and one which by its nature gives the painter his opportunity, when storms and tempests arise, to secure the necessary sittings; swarms of children, many of them charmingly pretty; no wonder that enough material has been found to keep us engaged these many years.

Of almost equal importance, too, is the costume worn, if dress as it is understood in England can be thus designated. Perhaps the attire of a fisherman comes as near deserving the name as anything we can show (in this country), for it is distinctive and characteristic of his calling. I can remember occasional lapses, which made one fear that this too was passing away with other old-fashioned and paintable things, and one awful moment when a hideous fashion in hats set in – a hard, black abomination in place of the usual soft sailorlike headgear or quaint old sou'-wester. But on the whole fishermen in their working dress, clad in jerseys or white duck frocks, and wearing their great sea-going boots, are far from being as unpicturesque as the male portion of our race seem to delight in making themselves. The women, too, have a charming instinct of dress; but at the risk of offending them I must confess to admiring the neat blouses

Stanhope Forbes:

and cotton aprons of everyday wear rather than the grandeur and finery of their Sunday toilettes. Against the dress of the little ones there is not a word to be said. Always neat and tidy, the mothers, with excellent taste, choose for great occasions either white or pale colours, which seen in the sunshine, massed together in those charming processions the Cornish galas, have an altogether delightful effect.

But we have lingered long enough at the gate of the meadow, as this field is called which we now enter, to find a whole encampment of studios clustered together on a slope overlooking the bay. At first we had been contented with improvising our workshops out of discarded net lofts, or any other available structure, but by degrees the more conventional studio has sprung into existence, and these were amongst the first of them. They were originally founded by one of the best friends the artists have had, Mr Arthur Bateman, a gentleman who came to live and paint at Newlyn in the early days of the colony, and who, out of a strong feeling of comradeship and a desire to help his friends by facilitating their work, purchased this field and dedicated it to the service of artists and of art.

Strange sights have been seen in that meadow, and a few years ago a visitor might have been astonished to see a group of Elizabethan gentlemen in doublets and hose chatting pleasantly with swarthy blacksmiths, whilst a little maiden in medaeval attire would lean over the steps and gossip with these gentry of another age. For it is the hour of the models' repose, and for a short period they have escaped from the hot studio to stretch their limbs and breathe the air.

As we leave one cannot repress a slight feeling of regret at the recollection of those pleasant days when the field was gay with crowds of visitors who had flocked thither for our yearly private view. It was, I think, Percy Craft who with me a good many years ago first introduced to Newlyn this fashion, and by degrees the custom grew until almost everyone adopted it, and the numbers of our visitors swelled from a handful of personal friends to that large crowd that

Stanhope Forbes:

each year filled the meadow, strolling from studio to studio, gazing at the pictures and getting a glimpse of our workshops and our ways.

But when fate in the person of Mr Passmore Edwards decreed that we should possess an art gallery, it became inevitable that the pictures could no longer be exhibited in this novel manner, and seeing the many advantages which the possession of a properly constructed exhibition room has conferred upon us, it were ungenerous to cavil at so small a matter. We have seen the building just before entering the village. Its exterior, with four walls bare of windows by the necessities of its construction, scarcely afforded much opportunity to its architect, but those panels of beaten copper on the facade are worth noticing. They are a product of the place, one of the latest developments of Newlyn art.

In the narrowest part of the little lane we stumbled along on our way through the village, there hangs a curiously fashioned sign, indicating that here an industrial class is held. A terrible din assails your ears, and, curious to find what occasions it, you enter a courtyard, and, climbing a steep ladder into an old net loft, find a room full of lads all busy hammering away at curiously shaped pieces of brass or copper. Originally started by that good friend of Newlyn, Mr Bolitho, with the cooperation of the artists, and chief amongst them Messrs. Gotch and Percy Craft, the idea was to find employment for the spare moments of fisherlads, and certainly a more admirable safety valve for their superfluous energy could not have been devised.

But to resume our ramble. All around us now are the houses in which at one time or another most of us have found a home. Newlyn is not very fortunately situated in this respect, for good lodgings are not plentiful, and at times the demand exceeds the supply. Built at a time when an invasion of painters was not foreseen, the village possesses few houses which can do more than accommodate the fishermen and their families who inhabit them; and this difficulty of procuring rooms has somewhat tended to check our

Stanhope Forbes:

expansion. Still there are comfortable and pleasant quarters to be found by searching, in which we have lived happily enough. Here is one old house endeared to many of us by the recollection of the old days when we lived there side by side. In its garden stands a wooden studio which I saw constructed, and afterwards shared with Percy Craft and at times with Chevalier Tayler.

Further on is a charming house, under whose hospitable roof a genial host and hostess have done so much to promote and encourage that feeling of good fellowship which has always existed among us – the home of Mr and Mrs Gotch. Indeed, this quarter of Newlyn is the very centre of the social life of the colony. Amongst the pleasantest of our recollections are the visits of those foreign painters, many of whom have made lengthy sojourns here, won by the charm of this fair English county, by the wild grandeur of its rugged coast, or by the softer beauty of its valleys and woodland glades. And the presence of those strangers, who, foreign only by race, are of our close kith and kin in their relationship of art, is of an importance beyond measure, for the value to artists of an interchange of views and ideas with their foreign brethren cannot be over-estimated. Cornwall has, indeed, been fortunate in attracting the artists of other lands. I remember finding in a house at St Ives where I was calling, four painters of four different nationalities. Indeed, so many of our transatlantic cousins have visited us, that who can tell to what extent we may not claim to have fostered those cordial relations which we are told now exist between the two nations?

But we have still much to see, so resume our wanderings and, prying into the little passages and courts which abound in Newlyn, obtain a glimpse of a fisherman's home life and ways. We shall find many another studio tucked away in odd corners, queer old ramshackle places, many of them exceedingly serviceable and admirably suggestive.

Leaving the village now, for a glance at the country around, we might follow the course of a charming little brook up the rich coombe or valley down which it trickles. It

Stanhope Forbes:

is difficult to think that this can be the same river that only a few years ago came roaring down this quiet valley, through the heart of the village, wreaking destruction and havoc around on the day of the memorable flood. Now we pass a church where Newlyn marriages take place, and another Newlyn school. We have still to climb that terrible hill that leads up into the higher land above to see the favourite haunts of our landscape painters. Wandering inland we may perhaps be overtaken by some of them spinning past, with canvas and brushes strapped to their bicycles, hurrying to their daily task; perhaps out on the moors, or in the heart of some quiet wood, catch sight of those little wooden shanties, excellent movable studios, which some have lately adopted.

Before turning homewards we might prolong our walk through the lovely valley of Lamorna, until we reach a group of farm buildings by the side of the road, where we stop to admire the very latest achievement of two distinguished artists, a sign hanging on the wall of a cottage, indicating by a most charming painting that refreshments can here be obtained for wearied cyclists.

And now we have seen Newlyn, and something of the lives of its painters, and have had a peep behind the scenes. I may be allowed to express the pride I feel in the successes of these my comrades and associates. For indeed the applause has not been stinted, and the Newlyn School can surely not complain of want of recognition.

X

The Mine Where the Bay Should Be

Some four or five miles westward from Mount's Bay is a modest little inlet formed by a break in the line of tall, chunky, sloping cliff face. But Porthcurno's modest, outward appearance belies its true character, combining the ancient and modern: for close to the beach is a mound on which perhaps are the ruins of a chapel credited with being a thousand years old. Nothing very much in that, I hear you comment. Yes, but ... nearby you can see a dozen thick telegraph cables disappearing into the sea carrying within them the facility of communication all over the world.

The first of the cables laid from Cornwall ran from Sennen Cove; that was to the Scilly Isles in 1869. From then on Porthcurno took over. Here the Cable Telegraph Company made its headquarters. Since then the work at this village can be said to have had an immense influence on the development of world communications in the century and a quarter that it has been training men for duty in far distant places.

In 1870 a cable was laid along the seabed to Malta, a thousand miles away, and this was the first stage of a project of monumental proportions, namely, to lay a cable to Australia. Within a year it had been extended as far as Singapore, and in November 1872, the first line was open to Australia, surely a monumental task requiring great courage and imagination. Two ships were engaged at a time when laying the cable, each of them carrying a cable *eighteen hundred miles long*! When one goes to Porthcurno today it looks no different to any other holiday beach, with sunbathers and bathers, and all, untouched by glamour.

The coastline of this western face of Cornwall is spectacular, but the reefs that edge it and the headlands that jut out from it, the complexity of the tides, and the vulnerability of a sailing vessel making a landfall after days of sunless weather without a fix, these things combined to make it a graveyard for fine ships, great and small, as grimly receptive as anywhere in the world.

However, undaunted by the scale of disasters imposed upon seamen in pursuit of earning a living, the miners took it upon themselves to work a copper mine *under the sea*. Surely, one would think, that was an anachronism in terms of endeavour if ever there was one … a mine, the sea – together? A mine *under the sea?* In the early forties of the last century a visit was paid to Botallack mine by traveller Wilkie Collins, who left us a copy of his account of it. Come now, let's join him, let's hear the thump of the waves as they break on our 'roof' of sea and see if we like it. Botallack mine is a mile north of Cape Cornwall.

Having heard that there was a disinclination to allow strangers to go down the mines my friend and I had provided ourselves with a proper introduction. We were told to go to the counting-house to present our credentials, and on our road there beheld the buildings and machinery of the mine, literally stretching down the precipitous face of the cliff, from the land at the top, to the sea at the bottom. Here we beheld a scaffolding perched on a rock that rose out of the waves – there, a steam-pump was at work raising gallons of water from the mine every minute, on a mere ledge of land halfway down the steep cliffside.

Chains, pipes, conduits, protruded in all directions from the precipice; rotten-looking wooden platforms, running over deep chasms, supporting great beams of timber and heavy coils of cable; crazy little boarded houses were built where gulls' nests might have been found in other places.

There did not appear to be a foot of level space anywhere, for any part of the workers to stand upon; and yet, there they were, fulfilling all the purposes for which they had been constructed, as safely and completely on rocks in the sea, and down precipices of land, as if they had been cautiously founded on the tracts of smooth, solid ground above.

The counting-house was built on a projection of earth about midway between the top of the cliff and the sea. When we got there, the agent, to whom our letter was addressed, was absent, but his place was supplied by two miners who came out to receive us. To one of them we mentioned our recommendation, and modestly hinted a wish to go down the mine forthwith. He looked upon us with a benevolent, paternal expression, and appeared to think we were nothing like strong enough or cautious enough to be trusted down the mine. 'Did we know,' he urged, 'that it was dangerous work?' 'Yes, but we didn't mind danger.'

'Perhaps,' he went on, 'we were not aware that we would perspire profusely, and be dead tired getting up and down the ladders.' 'Very likely, but we didn't mind that either.'

'Surely, you wouldn't like to strip and put on miners' clothes?' 'Yes! We should!' Each climbed into what looked like a flannel shirt that dropped down over his toes like a bedgown, and trousers that flowed in Turkish luxuriance over his feet, and drawers seemingly designed to fit men half their size.

In due course, we left the counting house and ascended the face of the cliff, then walked a short distance along the ledge, descended a little again, and stopped at a wooden platform across a deep gully. Here the miner pulled up a trap-door, and disclosed a perpendicular ladder leading down to a black hole, like the opening of a chimney. 'This is the shaft, I will go down first to catch you in case you tumble; follow me and hold tight.' This we did, having lit our candles.

The process of climbing down the ladders was not very pleasant. They were all quite perpendicular, and the footrests, many of them much worn away were slippery with water and copper-ooze; add to this the narrowness of the shaft, the dripping wet rock shutting you in, as it were, all round your back and sides against the ladder – the fathomless-looking darkness beneath – the light flaring immediately above you – the consciousness that if the rounds of the ladder broke you might fall one thousand feet or so of narrow tunnel in a moment – imagine all this and you may easily realise what are the first impressions when descending down a Cornish mine.

In due course, the miner told them they were now four hundred yards out under the Atlantic Ocean and that they must keep strict silence and listen.

After a few moments, a distant, unearthly noise becomes faintly audible – a long, low, mysterious moaning, that never changes, that is *felt* on the ear as well as *heard* by it – a sound that might proceed from some incredible distance, from some far invisible height – a sound unlike anything that is heard on the upper ground – a sound, so sublimely mournful and still, so ghostly and impressive when listened to in the subterranean recesses of the earth, that we continue instinctively to hold our peace, as if enchanted by it, and think not of communicating to each other the strange awe and astonishment which it has inspired in us both from the very first.

At last, the miner spoke again and told us that the sound we heard was the sound of the surf lashing the rocks a hundred and twenty feet above us and of the waves that were breaking on the beach beyond. When the sea was rough, he tells us, 'the noise was terrific and so bad that, not surprisingly, even the boldest men at work were afraid to continue their labour' – and so say all of us, I am sure.

XI

St Ives Bay

Allow me to let Neville Norway introduce us to St Ives as it was towards the end of the last century:

> There is such infinite variety in these Cornish fishing towns. Here is a huddled hump of houses tumbling one over the other in a cleft of precipices, but the fishing boats are hauled up in safety. It is a sweet and sunny place, a harbour full of clear blue water, the sandy shores of the wide bay curving round Phillack and Gwythian, past Godrevy Island, where the lighthouse gleams tall and white against a background of blue sea and so on past Portreath and Perranporth to the dim line of that grand northern coast which holds the finest scenery in Cornwall.
>
> Here nothing is grand, but soft and sunny and exquisite; and always some little fishing boats slipping in and out of the harbour or scudding to and fro in the big blue bay.

It sounds idyllic, and you might think that being sheltered from modern technical advances is a reason for St Ives still appearing to the visitor as above; so the following advertisement may well surprise you. It appeared in *1831*, over one hundred and fifty years ago. It is taken from the *Bristol Gazette* of 22 September 1831:

For St Ives and Hayle
With Passengers and Goods
The beautiful new Steam Packet
HERALD
John Vivian, Commander

This superior vessel is just arrived from Greenock where she was built, with engines of 100 horse power, but built purposely for the Trade, and no expense spared in fitting her for the comfort of Passengers and safety of Goods; she will lay at the Quay taking in Goods till Friday Evening and sail from Cumberland Basin on Saturday next.

The service was a weekly one, leaving Hayle every Wednesday on the tide and returning on Saturday. Single fares were, cabin £1 5s 0d (including steward's fee); deck 10s 6d; children under ten, half-price. The distance was about 150 sea-miles and a fair passage took twenty-two hours. The agent at Bristol was yet another John Harvey, again of no proved relationship with the Hayle family, though possibly a cousin. He lived at 66 Broad Quay Bristol, but soon after the service started he moved to the West of England Tavern (No 60) where he established a regular ticket-office.

On the far side of the bay was heavy industry in the shape of this Hayle Foundry, which closed its doors some few years ago. It was involved in heavy engineering, servicing the local mines, and smelting, and was formed in 1822.

A poignant picture of the price paid by the smelters was painted by the Reverend Warner, writing in 1809:

This busy scene of commercial bustle, with the gentle presence of the old church of the former village seen across its creek, nestling itself in trees, recalls association connected with the picturesque. This quiet scene is agreeably opposed by the animation of the creek which contains a pretty considerable fleet of trading ships from Bristol and Wales which bring iron and coal for the mines [St Ives Consul mine was in the vicinity], and load back with copper; as many of the proprietors find it less expensive than to manufacture it on the spot. This, however, is not the case with all the ore, a part of which is smelted at Hayle, and then rolled into flat sheets at the *pounding houses*, about three miles to the southward of this place.

The processes of roasting and refining the ore at Hayle, during which it passes through six or seven furnaces, are highly interesting; but the pleasure rising from a sight so curious to those not familiar with it, is greatly damped by the appearance of the workmen engaged on it.

Nothing indeed can be more shocking than this scene, as an humane and enlightened visitor has observed, so dreadfully deleterious are the fumes of arsenic constantly impregnating the air of these places, and so profuse is the perspiration occasioned by the heat of the furnaces, that those who have been employed at them but a few months become most emaciated figures, and in the course of a few years are generally laid in their graves. Some of the poor wretches who were ladling the liquid metal from the furnaces to the moulds, looked more like walking corpses than human beings.

How melancholy a circumstance to reflect upon, and yet to how few does it occur that in preparing the materials of those numerous utensils which we are taught to consider indispensable for our kitchens, several of our fellow creatures are daily deprived of the greatest blessing of life, and too seldom obtain relief; but in losing life itself.

*

From the clear blue water of the bay, mentioned earlier in another context, were drawn, in a spectacular manner, vast numbers of fish, fishing being, as already mentioned, with mining and agriculture, the traditional industries of Cornwall. St Ives not only had a treasure chest of prime fish to depend on, but also for further commercial gain and labour opportunities, the St Ives Consul mine was more or less on its doorstep. I propose now, with my readers' kind consent, to bring to your notice a word picture of the fascinating technique employed by the fishermen for 'trapping' the pilchard.

We have seen how it is done by Newlyn, now see how it is done by St Ives with the seine net: it is quite something and very different, and exciting. However, I have a feeling in my bones that our old friend, Harry Carter, is hovering near and I suggest we get him out of our way first; but the tale he brings is something quite new – that of having had a request from none other than the Revenue officer to help them capture, or destroy a large privateer which has done much damage in the St Ives Bay area. It was called the *Black Prince* and, Harry, now out of prison from France and with a large new boat with 20 guns, had no reason to refuse to help the officer.

'It was not a very agreeable business,' said Harry, but he really had no option as he would gain much from helping out the Revenue man. The privateer was from Dunkirk and had taken many prizes off the Cornish coast and had to be sunk or captured.

Harry sailed from Mount's Bay round Land's End, with another armed vessel in company, a lugger (Harry's new boat was a cutter). They stayed two or three days in St Ives bay, and then the *Black Prince* was sighted offshore on Christmas Day (1780) in the morning. Harry continues in his diary:

We, not having our proper crews on board, collected a few men together and went to sea in pursuit, soon coming up with him. There followed a running fight in rougher and rougher seas, lasting four or five hours. The lugger fired a shot that carried away our jib [writes Harry] and another shot on the hull, so we were in some difficulty, and bore up after the lugger, not knowing what was the matter with her running away.

We came up with her about five in the evening. The captain wanted to abandon her, but he hopefully made for Padstow, continuing pumping and bailing until about six when he hailed me saying, stand by him as he was going to quit her. So they hoisted their boate, but the sea being so big, and the men being confused, she kept on taking in water heavily so that they could not free her any more.

I got my boate out in the meantime and sent her alongside the lugger so that some of the men jumped overboard and my boate picked them up, and suddenly the lugger went down. I hove to the cutter, and laid her to, so that she drifted right over the place where the lugger went down. Some of the men got on board by virtue of ropes, some got hold of the jib tack, and some picked up the cutter's boat, so that we saved alive seventeen men, and fourteen drowned.

As Providence would have it, it was about full-moon, or certainly all must have been lost. There was a scene indeed, What cries! What screeches! What confusion was there! We stayed some little time cruising about the place, but were soon obliged to get the cutter under way.

Harry at one stage thought he was wounded, and was picked up by one of his officers and 'this was a great salvation, and that of God would not suffer me to do any more, for all so many hundreds of shot have flyed around me, I never received so much as a blemish in one of my fingers.'

Well, well! It might be thought that all those goings-on might excite the interest of the people of St Ives, but even if the battle between the cutter and the lugger had been closer in and more spectacular, the men and women of the town had much more important business to pursue: shoals of pilchards were come close inshore and were simply asking to be caught close in. What treasure! A million fish just asking to be caught! And markets as far away as the Mediterranean eager to claim them.

We have seen the way the fishermen of Newlyn went about the business of catching by employing a drift net. The men of St Ives employed a different method. Before recounting this very interesting activity, let me look with you at a contemporary's 1851 picture of the setting of this lovely area.

The town of St Ives is admirably situated at the end of a bay round which it forms a crescent, and is surrounded by sandhills bordered by cliffs. It has been compared to a Greek village. It is quite certain that the blue sky, the sea, the hills with their white sides, and the black rocks with their vigorous lines, compose, with the town seated in a hollow, a delightful picture. Like at Newlyn, the setting and the light drew many artists there.

On the quay stand the old buildings of an abandoned mine; farther on a church, protected from the sea by a stout wall, and surrounded by a cemetery, bravely offers to the waves its old stained glass windows which have many times been beaten by a storm. Unfortunately, St Ives does not gain by being seen more closely. The more beautiful its position is, the more do its narrow, winding streets appear made to sadden visitors and dispel illusions. It is a thorough fishing town. Nearly all the houses have stone steps outside leading to the first floors where the families live, while the ground floors are occupied by the fish cellars. The latter spread through the inhabited parts of the houses exhalations which are far from being agreeable, especially in the pilchard season; but the fishermen scent in this fish an odour quite as good as another – the fragrance of gain and prosperity.

The buildings intended to receive and prepare the catch attain considerable proportions at St Ives. The cellars, covered by a gallery supported by iron columns, open on to a square yard and resemble cloisters as much through their size as through the solidity of the architecture.

Let us now place ourselves into the hands of another contemporary for a vivid description of the extraordinary size and complexity of the operation which will catch up to a million and more fish in a couple of days and nights. We bid farewell for a while to Ambrose Esquiros, and welcome to Wilkie Collins (1851). He draws our attention to the fact that if a stranger in Cornwall went out to take his first walk along the cliffs towards the south of the county, in the month of August, that stranger could not advance far in any direction without witnessing what would strike him as a very singular and alarming phenomenon. He would see a man standing on the extreme edge of a precipice, just over the sea, gesticulating in a very remarkable manner with a bush in his hand, waving it to the right and left, brandishing it over his head, sweeping it past his feet; in short, apparently acting the part of a maniac of the most dangerous description. It would add considerably to the startling effect of this sight on the stranger if he were told, while beholding it, that the insane individual before him was paid for flourishing the bush at the rate of a guinea a week (mid-nineteenth century); and if he, thereupon, advanced a little to get a clearer view of the madman, and then observed on the sea below a well-manned boat, turning carefully to right and left exactly as the bush turned right and left, his mystification would probably be complete, and his ideas on the sanity of the inhabitants of the neighbourhood would at least be perplexed with grievous doubt.

Actually, the man with a bush was an important agent in the Pilchard Fishery of Cornwall; that he had just discovered a shoal of pilchards swimming towards the land; and that the men in the boat were guided by his gesticulations alone, in securing the fish on which they and all their countrymen on the coast depended for a livelihood.

The first sight from the cliffs of a shoal of pilchards advancing towards the land is not a little interesting. They produce on the sea the appearance of a shadow of a dark cloud. This shadow comes on and on until you can see the fish leaping and playing on the surface by hundreds at a time, all huddled close together, and all approaching so near to the shore that they can always be caught in fifty or sixty feet of water. Indeed, on certain occasions, when the shoals are of a considerable magnitude, the fish behind have been known to force the fish in front literally up to the beach, so that they could be taken in buckets, or even in the hand with the greatest of ease. It is said that they are thus impeld to approach the land by precisely that which impels the fishermen to catch them as they appear – the necessity for getting food.

With the discovery of the first shoal, the active duties of the look-out on the cliff edge began. Each village placed one or more of these men on watch all round the coast. They were called 'huers', and much depended on them; he was, therefore, not only paid his guinea a week while he was on watch, but received a bonus in terms of percentage of all the fish taken under his auspices.

The huer was placed at his post some little time before the shoals were expected to appear; at the same time, boats, nets and men were all made ready for action at a moment's notice.

The principal boat used was of at least fifteen tons burden, and carried a large net called the 'seine', which measured nine hundred feet in length and cost a hundred and seventy pounds – sometimes more. It was simply one long strip from sixty to eighty feet in breadth, composed of a very small mesh, and furnished all along its length, with lead at one side and corks the other. The men who cast this were called the 'shooters'.

The grand object was to enclose now the entire shoal. The heavy lead sank one end of the net perpendicular to the ground, and the corks buoyed up the other to the surface of the water. When the net had now been dragged all round the fish, the two extremities (now together) were made fast, the shoal being then imprisoned within an oblong barrier of network surrounding it on all sides. The great art is to let as few pilchards escape as possible while this process was being completed.

Whenever the huer observed from above that they were startled, and were separating at any particular point, to that point he waves his bush and thither the boat is steered and there the net is shot at once. In whatever direction the fish attempted to get out to sea again, they were thus immediately met and thwarted with extraordinary skill. This labour completed, the silence of intense expectation that had hitherto prevailed among the spectators on the cliff-top, was broken. There was a great shout of joy on all sides – the shoal was secured!

At this time in the operation the 'seine' was now regarded as a great reservoir of fish. It might remain in the water a week or more. To secure it against being moved from its position should a gale come on, it was warped by two or three ropes to points of land in the cliff, and was, at the same time, contracted in circuit by its opposite ends being brought together and fastened tight over a length of several feet. While these operations were going on, another boat, another set of men, and another net (but different to a seine) were approaching the scene of action.

This new net was called a 'tuck', smaller than the seine,

inside which it was now to be let down for the purpose of bringing the fish closely collected to the surface. This boat was first of all rowed inside the seine net and laid close to the big seine boat which remained stationary outside.

I am getting rather lost as I write this description, and I warrant my kind readers are, too; so let us move on to the scene on shore with everything ready for the hauling of the mass of fish to the surface. Everybody is madly excited. The merchants, to whom the boats and nets belonged and by whom the men were employed, joined the huer on the cliff: all their friends followed them; boys shouted, dogs barked, and every little boat in the place put off, crammed with idle spectators. Old men and women hobble down to the beach to wait for the news. The noise, the bustle, the agitation increased every moment. Soon the shrill cheering of the boys was joined by the seiners. There they stood, six or eight sunburnt stalwart fellows ranged in a row in the seine boat, hauling with all their might at the tuck net, and roaring the regular nautical yo-heave-ho chorus. Higher and higher rose the net, louder and louder shouted the boys and the idlers. The merchant forgot his dignity and joined them: the huer, so calm and collected hitherto, lost his self-possession and waved his cap triumphantly. Let now our companion, Wilkie Collins, take over as he joins in the shouts, Hooray! Hooray! Yo-hoy, yo-hoy! Pull away boys! Up she comes! Here they are! Here they are!

The water boils and eddies: the tuck net rises to the surface and one teeming, convulsed mass of shining, glancing, silvery scales; one compact crowd of thousands of fish, each one of which is madly endeavouring to escape, appears in an instant!

The noise before was as nothing compared with the noise now. Boats as large as barges are pulled up in hot haste all round the net; baskets are produced by the dozen; the fish are tipped up into them and shot out like coals in a sack, into the boats. Before long, the men are up to their ankles in pilchards; they jump up on to the rowing benches and work on until the boats are filled with fish as full as they can hold, and the gunwhales are within two or three inches of the water. Even yet the shoal is not exhausted; the tuck net must be let down again and left ready for a fresh haul while the boats are slowly rowed to the shore.   As soon as the fish are brought to land, one set of men, bearing capacious wooden shovels, jump in among them, and another set bring large hand-barrows close to the side of the boat into which the pilchards are thrown with amazing rapidity. This operation proceeds without ceasing for a moment. As soon as one barrow is ready to be carried to the salting-house another is waiting to be filled. When this labour is performed at night, the scene becomes doubly picturesque. The men with the shovels, standing up to their knees in pilchards, working energetically; the crowd stretching down from the salting-house, across the beach, and hemming in the boat all round; the uninterrupted succession of men hurrying backwards and forwards with their barrows through a narrow way, kept clear from them in the throng; the glare of the lanterns giving light to the workmen and throwing red flashes as they fly incessantly from the shovels over the side of the boat, all combine to produce such a series of striking contrasts, such a moving picture of hustle and animation, as no attentive spectator can ever forget.

Having watched the progress of affairs on the shore, we next proceed to the salting-house, a quadrangular structure of granite well roofed in all round the sides but open to the skies in the middle. Here we must prepare ourselves to be bewildered by incessant confusion and noise; for here are assembled all the women and girls of the district, piling up the pilchards on layers of salt, at three pence an hour; to which remuneration a glass of brandy and a piece of bread and cheese are hospitably added every sixth hour by way of refreshment. It is a service of some little hazard to enter this place at all. There are men rushing out with empty barrows in almost perpetual succession.

As the filled barrows are going into the salting-house, we observe a little urchin running by the side of them, and hitting their edges with a long cane in a constant succession of smart strokes, until they are carried through the gate, when he quickly returns to perform the same office for the next series that arrive. The object of this apparently unaccountable proceeding is soon practically illustrated by a group of children hovering about the entrance to the salting-house, who every now and then dash resolutely up to the barrows and endeavour to seize as many fish as they can take away at one snatch. It is understood that this is their privilege, to keep as many pilchards as they can get in this way by dexterity, in spite of a liberal allowance of strokes aimed at their hands: and their adroitness richly deserves its reward. Vainly does the boy, officially instructed with the administration of the cane, strike the sides of the barrow with malignant perseverance and smartness – fish are snatched away with lightning rapidity and pickpocket neatness of hand. The hardest rap over the knuckles fails to daunt the assailant while howling with pain he dashes up to the next barrow that passes him, with unimpaired resolution. In an hour they could collect ten or a dozen fish each.

Now, while we have a chance, while the doorway is accidentally clear for a few moments, let us enter the salting-house, and approach the noisiest and most amusing of all the scenes which the pilchard fishery presents. First of all we pass a great heap of fish lying in a recess inside the door, and an equally large heap of coarse, brownish salt lying in another. Then we advance further, and get out of the way of everybody, behind a pillar; and see a whole congregation of the fair sex screaming, talking and – to their honour be it spoken – working at the same time, round a compact mass of pilchards which their nimble hands have already built up to a height of three feet, a breadth of more than four and a length of twenty.

Here we have every variety of the 'female type' displayed before us, ranged round an odoriferous heap of salted fish. Here, we see crones of sixty and girls of sixteen; the ugly, the lean, the comely and the plump; the sour-tempered and the sweet – all squabbling, singing, jesting, lamenting, and shrieking at the very top of their shrill voices for more fish and more salt; both of which are brought in small buckets by a long train of children running backwards and forwards with unceasing energy and inextricable confusion: but, universal as the uproar is, the work never flags, the hands move as fast as the tongues. There may be no silence, no discipline, but there is also no idleness, no delay. Never was threepence an hour more joyously or more fairly earned than here!

After the floor has been swept clean, a thin layer of salt is spread on it, and covered with pilchards laid partly edgeways, and close together. Then another layer of salt is spread on it, smoothed fine with the palm of the hand, is laid over the pilchards, and then more pilchards are placed upon that; and so on until the heap rises to four feet or more.

Nothing can exceed the ease, quickness and regularity with which this is done. Each woman works in her own small area without reference to her neighbour; a bucketful of salt and a bucketful of fish being shot out in two little piles under her hands for her own special use. All proceed in their labour, however, with such equal diligence and skill that no irregularities appear in the various layers when they are finished. They run as straight and smooth from one end to the other, as if they were constructed by machinery. The heap, when finished, looks like a long, solid, neatly made mass of dirty salt, nothing being now seen of the pilchards but the extreme tips of their noses or tails just peeping out in rows up the side of the pile.

The fish will remain in salt in bulk for five or six weeks. During this period, a quantity of oil, salt, and water drips from them into wells cut in the centre of the stone floor on which they are placed. After the oil has been collected and clarified it will sell well enough to pay off the whole expense of the wages, food and drink given to the seiners. The salt and water remaining, and offal of all sorts found with it, furnish a valuable manure. Nothing in the pilchard itself, or in connection with it, runs to waste.

After the fish have been taken out of 'bulk', they are washed clean in salt water and packed in hogsheads [huge wooden casks, each holding some 2,500 pilchards or more]. These are then sent to an appropriate port for export, Penzance, for instance, in small coastal traders to the Mediterranean, Italy and Spain providing the two great foreign markets. Home consumption is comparatively very small. It is rather odd that it was the Roman Catholic countries that depended on a Protestant country for the vital ritual supply of fish on Fridays.

The fish reserved for Cornwall were generally cured by those who purchased them. Some idea of the huge multitude of fish caught on the shores of Cornwall can be gauged from the fact that at the small fishing cove of Trereen [close to the Logan Rock] 600 hogsheads were taken in little more than one week during August, 1850. This amounts to no less than *1,440,000* pilchards caught by inhabitants of one little village alone, at the commencement of the season. At St Ives, 27,000 hogsheads [remember, 2,500 fish in each] were exported annually.

Such is the picture of one of Cornwall's three vital industries, fishing, agriculture and mining. For my part, I find it an absorbing interesting story – but if there are any of my readers, and I'm sure there must be some, who've had more than enough of my fishy, fishy tale, to them I offer sympathy and regrets.

XII

Newquay Bay

This most beautiful bay, whose perimeter boasts no fewer than four wonderful beaches of firm golden sand, any one of which could serve elsewhere to create a resort of its own; yes, this most beautiful bay is now a 'fun' bay giving enjoyment to thousands of holidaymakers every summer.

Its setting, too, is lovely. Let me borrow, from one spectator, his description of the panorama one afternoon a century ago:

On Newquay Head a strong breeze is blowing off the land and all the sea in that wide bay which lies between the great headland of Trevose, ten miles away up the coastline, and Pentire to the westward, is ruffled over with white splashes, which come and go and change perpetually upon a bed of that glorious dark colour which is neither green nor blue. The coastline is half-veiled by a little haze, shadowy, faint, and opalescent, so that one can hardly see where the cliff meets sea till some sudden flash of white surges up from a breaking wave and goes again in haze as the swells come back and the broken water passes. Far away the dim line stretches, past Port Island with its blowhole spouting high as each wave rushes up the gulley, past Watergate, where huge dark caverns open upon golden sands, past Mawgan Porth, that loveliest of coves, where towering headlands enclose a beach as firm and even as a ballroom floor, past Bedruthan Steps, its strange rock forms all mingled and lost in the fine dim shadow, till at Trevose, the land ends suddenly and nothing further east is visible.

In the opposite direction, great rollers are curling in

across the mile wide Bay of Fistral, torn into clouds of flying spray as they curve and break and scatter into whirlpools of lasting foam. Often when the afternoon sets towards evening, there are seals diving and swimming in quiet spots around this headland. [1898]

Over a hundred years ago the scene in Newquay bay was rather different. Instead of the bay catering for today's wind-surfers, water-skiers, speedboats, catamarans, there might have been a dozen or more schooners in the harbour taking away iron ore from the Perranporth district, and grain from all the surrounding district. It was a scene of great activity. The iron ore was brought in wagons and carts which was then discharged down a shute opposite the Red Lion. It was then run out along the quays to the vessels. The quays were not long to accommodate all the vessels, and those awaiting their turn pulled up on the sandy beach within the harbour. China clay was also shipped, but before the railway was built (1875) all the clay came in huge wagons from St. Dennis.

Incoming vessels brought coal, guano, and bone manure, limestone and salt (for salting pilchards). The limestone was burnt in the district. One kiln was situated at the bend of the road going down South Quay Hill to the harbour. This kiln was always alight.

Friday was the day when the grain was brought in by the farm wagons. On that day, Red Lion Square was a scene of considerable liveliness. The vessel to be loaded was drawn up close under the cliff and the grain shot from the gallery through square wooden shutes into the hold, and later it was loaded into sacks because of the danger of a shifting cargo.

Newquay people owned and captained a dozen or more schooners. It was the custom that the ownership of one quarter of the shares of any vessel carried with it the right of captaincy, provided that the seamanship of the person was adequate.

Each boat carried five or six persons including the captain, and there were quite a number of seafaring people among the population, not fewer than a hundred (out of about five hundred). In addition to these a number of men were connected with the working of the boats; hobblers who discharged and loaded the vessels, and piloted boats in and out of the harbour.

Ship-building, boat-building, repairing and sail-making gave employment to a number of men. The boats were built for Newquay owners. There were three yards where they were built – one was situated in the cove within the harbour under the Retreat, another occupied Giant's Cove at the Island end of the Town beach. There were also two at Porth and one in the Gannel.

The dangers of seafaring did not allow our town to escape, and oft times did the women have their men in the prime of life snatched from among them. Nancy Glanville's husband had built a sailing boat and had gone with his only son to test her sailing qualities. In rounding the Headland on their way back to the harbour the boat was overturned by a sudden squall and both were drowned. Nancy was left with five little girls, a terrible problem to confront a widow, but like another woman in similar circumstances she worked and accomplished her herculean task of rearing the family.

One evening the news came that Captain Will Clemens' vessel was wrecked, and he and all the crew drowned. 'How well I remember,' wrote a woman at the time, 'the cry of agony from that household of six girls and a boy; I never understood the full meaning of the word "orphan" before that sad event when the eldest daughter cried, "We are orphans!" ' Their mother, a very delicate woman, had died not long before, and the eldest child, a girl of sixteen, took the terrible responsibility of mothering the family, and well, indeed, did she bring them up. Eventually the boy sailed his own vessel, two of the daughters married captains of vessels, and the youngest married a well-to-do farmer.

Another woman, whose husband was captain of a trading vessel, was left with five children. He died from injuries on board when only forty years of age. One day a lady called to see his widow and said, among other things, 'But Mary, you don't seem poor. Your little family are clean, and their clothing whole!' 'Yes,' Mary replied sharply, 'and always will be so long as I have three-half-halfpence – a penny to buy soap and a halfpenny for thread.'

Evidence of the closeness of this seafaring community to one another is exemplified in a moving account of the arrival of the first lifeboat especially designed for Newquay. It is by a Newquay woman; her name was S. Teague Husband, and we can be very grateful for the picture of Newquay life which she has left us.

The lifeboat

The hazards of a seafaring life have always called forth the best in the human character. Not only does it require physical courage to endure the hardships, but moral courage is also needed to enable the sailor to put up with the discomforts and monotony and the hazards of his calling.

But it is when danger comes, when the sea takes on its deadly aspect to the mariner that we see the unselfish side of the seafaring nature.

There was certainly something praiseworthy when our men, in the old days, voluntarily watched the coasts, and without incentives from the outside world, or any promise of remuneration went forth in boats, not made especially for the purpose to save those in danger. The only boats available were the long narrow gigs which possessed only one of the characteristics of the modern lifeboat, that of a fair speed.

At last, however, came the lifeboat specially designed for the purpose it was intended to serve. Great was the excitement in the town and many were the speculations among the young as to the shape, size and capabilities of this wonderful new boat.

At that time (1860) there was not a family but had relatives engaged in the seafaring life, so the enthusiasm displayed was of a mutual as well as of a personal character.

We watched George Burt's six great horses go out of the town one morning to fetch home the wonderful treasure, and the talk all day was about the boat and its approximate time of arrival. In the evening, all who could walk trooped out as far as Narrowcliff. In those days this was considered a long distance as there were no houses beyond the foot of Marky's Hill [Marcus Hill now].

As it was dark we could only listen for the sound of the wheels, but soon the word was passed along – 'She's coming!' The thrill caused in all hearts as each one echoed the words, still lives in the memory. The horses were stopped. We crowded round; we cheered; we touched her; and with feelings almost akin to reverence we felt we were welcoming a true friend. Then the signal was given for starting and we formed in procession and marched into the town to the lifeboat house.

A lifeboat house had already been built, a little beyond the coastguard houses in Fore Street. When the boat had been drawn to the boat house there came the excitement of backing her into the house, and in the dim light of lanterns she seemed a huge thing to be put through such a narrow entrance, but Georgie had a way of his own in talking to his horses, and they certainly understood his language, and after various backings she was eventually lodged in her house.

On the evening of the christening and launching, she was taken down into the harbour and got ready for the ceremony. By mutual consent the honour of christening this, our first lifeboat, was accorded to Mrs Willie Mitchell. The young squire looked very pleased as he led his young wife down the old walk into Quay Hill from the Fort grounds, and stood hat in hand during the whole ceremony. A hymn was sung, a prayer offered and then Mrs. Mitchell stepped forward to the boat and said, 'I name you *Joshua*. When you go forth on the mighty waters, may you like Joshua of old, as your name implies, be the saviour of men.' Then came the first launching.

We watched the men as they put on their cork jackets for the first time and took their seats; after which she floated from her carriage. This caused great excitement, but there was still more to follow. She was taken across the harbour to the steps of the North Pier and all the moveable tackle taken out. Long ropes were passed under her and made secure, and the other ends of the ropes were handed up to men on the pier. These set to work with a will and soon she was upset and we had the pleasure of seeing all the crew floundering about in the water. The boat righted herself beautifully, and several of the men scrambled back into her again, but others kept floating about. I heard one, I think it was Bill Burt, call up to the men on the pier and say, 'I know nothing about swimming – but it's all right. I find I can't sink with this jacket on.'

Everyone seemed fully satisfied with this her first testing, and felt that with such an efficient boat a new era in rescue work had dawned on Newquay, and there would be far less dread now than formerly when the winter gales came.

By now, dear reader, if you are still with me, you will have become aware of the latent danger that hovers, in varying degree, over a seafaring community that lives with the sea and seamen, (in the days of sail). The facts, to the outsider, do not linger more than an instant, on the surface of emotion, whereas the community is subconsciously aware of the shadow in the back of the mind when the winds blow and the great waves tumble gleefully.

I am now going to submit to you brief notes on events at and around Newquay relating to the hazards affecting the concern of local families. Read them carefully through, and by the end, I warrant, you will find yourself feeling touched by unease at the lifestyle of the bay in relation to family life.

1625 Nicholas Jefferye, a seafaring man and master of a shippe of Dartmouth lost and cast away on the 6th day November at St. Columb the Lower, Towan, Newquay, with three others of his company being found no more.

1843 Off St Agnes Captain Darke took a floating 75-foot whale in tow, landing it on beach at Barrowfields. Girth forty-five feet and lower jaw, nineteen feet. Captain purchased at auction sale for £15. Oil melted out on beach and 100 gallons taken first day. Inhabitants remembered odour.

Juliana: Nearly all sails and spars lost, was drifting to shore. Evening, and too rough for assistance. Inhabitants, pilots and coastguards held consultation resulting in lighted tar barrels being placed on each pierhead. Ship made for lights and entered harbour amid cheering of people in which crew joined.

Erato of Cork: Same night as Juliana. Lost spars and canvas and drifting to shore. Had 200 pigs and their owners on board. When within short distance of Mawgan beach saw pier lights toward which they managed to steer, safely entering harbour.

Agnes: Rudder carried away, was drifting ashore. Crew rowed to Carter's Rock, being there for twenty-four hours without food or shelter. Vessel struck Chick Rock and went to pieces. Mr. Hoblyn of Perran sent a man on horse to St Ives, boat proceeded to rescue, crew brought in here (Newquay).

1847, Marchioness of Abercorne: A barque with crew of 29 stranded on Crantock Beach (Newquay). Tribute paid to Captain Darke of *Rose*, Captain Johns of *Liberty* and a mate who pulled through raging sea and with rope connected ship with beach. Vessel purchased by merchants of Padstow, and taken there.

1849, Model: Loaded first consignment, 30 tons of lead ore, from East Wheal Rose mine, thus marking the opening of railroad from harbour to mine. Contractors and farmers so satisfied at the successful outcome, export of bullocks and sheep, that they had dinner and spent enjoyable evening at Clemen's Hotel.

1852, Queen Victoria: As vessel was running on beach, crew of four men and ship's boy left in ship's boat which was capsized, the only survivor, the boy, came ashore on an oar.

1854, December: There were 21 vessels in the harbour at one time, many of them being windbound.

To see the deserted harbour now it is difficult to realise that in 1889 one hundred and seven ships sailed in and out of the bay, and that the imports for the year were 9,000 tons, and exports 5,500 tons. Seventy families, fathers and sons, were engaged in the shipping trade, and at one time there were twelve ships in the little harbour. There was an average of four a week either coming in or going out.

*

Padstow Bay, is twelve miles up the coastline, to the north; twelve miles of tall, proud, and, be it said, potentially vicious rock, line the path from Newquay to Padstow.

XIII

Port Isaac to Padstow

Port Isaac – Port Quinn – Port Gaverne – Hell and Padstow Bays

The bay next to Padstow is Port Isaac, next to that Portquin and Port Gaverne. Samuel Drew in his *History of Cornwall*, writing in 1822 says:

> The principal village in this parish (of St Endelyon) is Port Isaac, in which a pilchard fishery has of late years been established, and in which has been a small market on Fridays for butcher's meat and a few other articles.
>
> At this inlet, coals are imported from Wales for the supply of the neighbouring inhabitants, and from it the principal export is slate raised in the Delabole quarries and brought hither as to the nearest port. Port Guin (sic) or as it is generally pronounced, Perguin, is said to have been formerly a large fishing town, but this declined in the same proportion that its rival Port Isaac rose.

Nearby is the monstrously huge slate quarry of Delabole and it was to serve this that the little havens were in being. I must tell you that a visit to this area today, far away from everywhere that it is, is well worth making, for though there are only very few signs of life (large empty fish cellars can still be seen) the shades of the past one feels around one in a strangely respectful way.

And let me say – the inn at Port Gaverne has an atmosphere, of warm and friendly hospitality from the past, to a degree that is positively inspiring, and rare indeed: so, with that treasure, bid farewell to Port Gaverne and welcome to Padstow.

Hell and Padstow Bays

Padstow is a very ancient place on the west bank of the Camel estuary. It is ten miles, as the gull flies, from Newquay. The harbour has been an important one, being one of only four on the west coast that provided shelter for the larger coastal vessels from westerly gales. It had a constant trade with Ireland, St Petroc landing in Padstow in the sixth century with sixty disciples.

It is believed that it was here that he founded a monastery occupying a site which Prideaux Place now occupies. St Petroc became the most important saint in Cornwall, and his reputation for power and sanctity has never been equalled.

Around his church at Padstow an area of sanctuary developed (where a man, sought by authority for an offence, could not be apprehended). This remained thus until the Reformation. Because of this Padstow in the Middle Ages was shunned as being a nest of evil-doers: right or wrong as that may be, there can be no doubt about the evil-doing of the Doom Bar, which was, and is still, a huge under-water bank of sand which blockaded the entrance to Padstow harbour except for a narrow gap at the base of Stepper Point.

It was sometime in the sixteenth century that the hazard first appeared. The sand came suddenly in a storm, so we are led to believe, and many houses were engulfed and lost.

The same story is told elsewhere in Cornwall, but at Padstow it was all due to a mermaid whom a Padstow man, thinking she was a fish, shot with an arrow: the mermaid, with her dying breath, cursed the town, and flung sand at it with the result that we can see at low tide the river outside the harbour being full of banks of brilliant yellow sand through which small boats can make their way, but which can be lethal to visiting vessels unfamiliar with the hazard when the tide is up. Since then, it has been the unwelcome cause of Padstow Bay gaining a reputation for being, until the age of sail was over, a ruthless killer of innocent vessels. This was made worse by the fact that men's lives — the men manning the lifeboat — exposed themselves, voluntarily, to the clash of leaving the family supper at the sound of the rockets going up and facing, perhaps, death. Here is the true picture of such a situation which brings it to life. It is told by the late Claude Berry of Padstow, in an interview with a lifeboatman, Edward Kane.

But first, let me put before you a striking verse which brings to life the horror of being on board a vessel as it sinks, and this happens to Edward Kane not so very long after leaving his peaceful supper at home in the kitchen:

She is sinking

Again she plunges! Hark, a second shock
  Tears her strong bottom on the marble rock
Down on the vale of death, with dismal cries
  The fated victims shud'ring, roll their eyes
In wild despair, while yet another stroke
  With deep convulsions rends the solid oak:
Till, like the mine, in whose infernal cell
  The lurking demons of destruction dwell,
At length, asunder torn, her frame divides
  And crashing spreads in ruin o'er the tides.

And now, let us share a moment with the late Claude Berry as he recalls, with Edward Kane, sailor and lifeboatman, the events on that night, 11 April 1900, one of the worst disasters in lifeboat history.

That evening 86 years ago, Kane was sitting in his little kitchen near the quayside at Padstow, cobbling a pair of shoes belonging to one of his children. No interior scene in the West Country could have been more homely and tranquil – the mellow lamplight, the shining crockery, the friendly shadows, and the father of the family bent over a familiar task.

Outside, the wind blew gustily, but not at gale force. Inside the quiet was only broken by the hammer blows, until the door was suddenly thrown open, and an excited voice cried, Edward the rockets have gone off! Without a word Kane dropped his hammer and shoe, seized his coat and hat, rushed out to join his comrades who were hurrying to Hawker's Cove to take their places in two lifeboats.

An hour or two later, Edward Kane and others were struggling for dear life in the wide expanse of water at the harbour entrance.

Kane's was the first body found, in the grey light of early morning under the cliffs of Hell Bay. Not far away was Padstow's steam lifeboat *James Stevens*, pride of the R.N.L.I. fleet. She had been driven into a cave and looked nothing so much as an enormous tin can – badly battered. Along the same reef of rocks lay two other victims of the storm: Padstow's rowing lifeboat, the *Arab* and the Lowestoft trawler *Peace and Plenty* which the two lifeboats had gallantly and vainly tried to reach before she was driven onto the rocks.

Three of the trawler's crew had been drowned. The other five, badly mauled by the' rocket life-saving apparatus at Trebetherick. Of the steam lifeboat's crew of eleven, only three had reached shore alive.

Thanks largely to the superb skill of the coxswain, Samuel Brown, the rowing lifeboat had been run into a small creek, and all her crew had swarmed over the rocks to safety. During their exhausting fight to reach the trawler a huge sea had broken over the *Arab* and washed eight of the men, with their oars, overboard. The oars were lost but the men miraculously struggled back to their places with only three oars intact.

It was a question now, not of reaching the trawler, but averting disaster to their own boat and themselves. When the boat struck a jagged shoulder of the reef, only one oar was unbroken. The rudder was smashed to matchwood; the boat's side was stove in. It was the end of the *Arab*.

Earlier on, the Arab had set off to intercept the distressed trawler which was being swept over the Doom Bar, by a direct thrust through a channel at the back of the Bar. The *James Stevens*, the other lifeboat (with Edward Kane in it) had steamed out to sea and was going to reach the trawler from that direction. The ground sea had never been worse, and more than once people on shore held their breath as the lifeboat's masthead light was lost to view in the trough of a great wave. Coxswain Grubb was handling the boat superbly. He had brought her safely round and was heading for the trawler and the *Arab* when a big breaker caught *James Stevens* on the quarter. She turned a complete somersault, pitching all but her engine-room crew into the water. Only three of them reached the shore alive. One of these told Claude Berry long afterwards that as he was struggling in the waves he heard the voice of only one of his comrades. It was Coxswain Grubb's – a despairing cry, 'Oh, Jimmy! Jimmy!' Jimmy was his son. Both were drowned.

Well, that is the story – eleven lives lost, two lifeboats and a trawler: and soon there were three new lifeboats at the Padstow Station, and never have ships in distress along that coast signalled in vain for assistance – and they never will.

ENDPIECE

The Watchful Eye of M. Alphonse Esquiros

One morning in August 1862, there arrived in Falmouth Bay a visitor from Brittany. His name was Esquiros, and he was the guest of a Cornish friend, Robert Were Fox, a well-known shipping agent and a member of the Royal Society. In Falmouth Fox was living in one of Cornwall's most beautiful residences, Grove Hill. From this base Esquiros contrived to observe the habits and lifestyle of the Cornishman at work and play, to a quite extraordinary degree. From him we get a fascinating picture of Cornwall's social history at that time, viewed by this keen-eyed visitor. Normally when we read of Cornwall's past it is only in general terms with which we are generally familiar. But Esquiros broadens our vision and fills us with human detail.

Join with me, now, to meet this friendly Frenchman of more than a hundred years ago, and ask him to tell us of some of his conclusions that he takes away with him, but which we can, with his approval, intercept before they are lost to us. We can imagine him looking out to sea across the Bay, and pondering over the pictures in his mind of Cornish life which he will shortly take home with him.

About miners, for instance. We have read, all of us, a lot about the great Cornish industry which was mining the tin and the copper and the lead that nature has left for us to retrieve from the depths of the earth, to our commercial advantage. Yes, the miners … but what of their home life, their working conditions, the role of their women folk? Esquiros will tell us:

The Cornish miners are a select race; at first glance you can distinguish them from the farm labourers, for they are so greatly noted by their stature and by an air of reflection and self-confidence. This physical and moral superiority results from the nature of their work which develops their strength, but exercises the judgement still more, as well as all the mental faculties.

The children of the miner generally attend school till the age of ten or twelve. After that age they enter the mine, where they at first work on the surface, and when they have become adult and strong, they gradually descend under ground. At the end of some time they know the value of different ores, and the manner of finding them. It has been said of the Cornish miners that they possess the mathematics of a mole. Endowed with a species of instinct and an admirable judgement, they find means to solve problems which seem to demand all the calculations of geometry. What height would this penetration attain if it were aided by study? When at home, the miner devotes himself to his garden. His house, which he often builds with his own hands, is not at all bad looking. Its furniture is plain; but you generally find two things which constitute the pride of an English home – stairs covered by a neat carpet, and very clean windows hung with curtains. Towards strangers he is kind and hospitable, though he is rather coarse in his manner.

His mode of living is simple. He never eats meat except on holidays. It is impossible to form an idea of a miner's kitchen without entering one. In the sheds of Dolcoath mine, there is a room in which the miners dry their clothes, and cook their dinner in an oven. This dinner consists of a turnip pie, or a little quantity of flour and currants mixed together and browned with a red hot plate. Along the coast the miners add fish to this frugal fare. If their fare is poor they have but few wants, and they enjoy an advantage inestimable in their sight – independence.

Sleeping little, at work mostly in the hours of darkness, they walk about during the day alone or with their wives. The life of miners would not be properly appreciated if we neglected their wives. The girls like the boys work in the mine from an early age. Their task is, as we have already seen, to break and prepare the ore. Wielding the hammer, and the rake, expands their shoulders and develops their form; hence they are generally well made, and are aware of the fact. They are called balmaidens

At the time of their daily avocations they are clean and neatly dressed; if by accident any of them have shoes uncleaned, they hide them with a shamefaced look under their too short skirts when a stranger visits the works. When they leave the mine they hastily repair, but artistically, the disorder which washing the ore has produced in their toilette: they then go across the fields in groups.

These groups offer many contrasts: the girls laugh, sing and tease the lads; the children play, while the old miners walk in silence, thinking of their supper. As they pass the cottages built along the roadside, the happy band naturally grows smaller, and those who live farther from the mine continue their walk in solitude.

The girls have worked all day for a very small wage, generally for seven or eight pence. Sometimes this money is honourably employed to support an old mother, or else proportionately to augment a whole family; but only too often this small sum is used to satisfy coquetry. In vain do the parents strive to combat this fatal inclination: the girls leave the cottage plainly dressed, but, under the nearest hedge they take out of their pocket a veil, a brooch, or some other ornament. These work-women of the mines have an inveterate foe in the packman – the name given to the pedlar who sells everything; sugar, tea, coffee, but more especially feminine finery. As he returns every fortnight he is also called Johnny Fortnight. This man tempts the girls in their weak point, vanity. As he does not ask for cash payments the bargain is soon concluded. If a girl is on the eve of marriage the packman persuades her that she wants a wedding outfit. She can pay this debt hereafter out of her husband's wages, and the transaction will be kept secret, for Johnny Fortnight represents himself as a model of discretion.

It is always the same story, the compact of the maiden who sells herself to the fiend. She falls into the power of this man who threatens to reveal everything if she does not keep her engagements, or refuses the goods he offers her afterwards. It is true that the miners have recourse to the same means to procure their Sunday clothes. You cannot recognise the ordinary mining population on a Sunday. On this day the men wear black coats, their wives silk dresses and bonnets with flowers.

Elegance being one of the fruits of civilisation, everybody wants to acquire it, as an external sign of an honourable and laborious life. The English only understand an equality that aspires and wishes to rise, and to this they make great sacrifices, hence, in spite of the great differences of rank and fortune, Great Britain is the country in which dress is most uniform and makes the nearest approach to luxury.

By contrast, let us take a look inside the house of a family farm:

The farms were generally of small size compared with those in English counties. The buildings were formed of large stones whose texture varies according to the geological character of the district, but in every case they looked very substantial. In them resided a family, generally very numerous, in which were displayed all ages, from grandfather to new-born babe. Their mode of living was extremely simple; the labourers dining at the same table with the family. They would have salt meat or fish, dumplings and boiled potatoes, and this would be repeated again and again. The farmers, as well as the labourers, would only drink water or tea, except at harvest time when they would have a little beer. In each room there was an air of comfort and cleanliness.

The sons of the family were often well educated, and the girls were active and coquettish. It was they who did the honours of the house to strangers with a modesty that had nothing awkward about it. In a sense, at that time in Cornwall, there were no 'peasants' left. London fashions were found in the most humble farms, and girls could be seen milking cows in a steel-hooped dress. All their dressing did not prevent them working well.

In some of the farms, there were as many as thirty or forty

oxen being fattened at once. At the same time, the stables, poultry yard and dairy had to be looked after, and much else.

In contrast now, we will enter the house of one of the Cornish gentry. In Cornwall the landed gentry live on the estate. They like to do that, and watch for themselves the running of the estate and the agricultural quest for the means for better husbandry.

Our good friend, M. Esquiros, informs us that

In France, rich persons pass a few summer months at their château, and then return to Paris to seek government offices or to indulge in winter amusements.

In England where there are few places to give away, and where London is not a capital of pleasures, things happen very differently. What are called provincial manners among us are nowhere found in the United Kingdom. In the counties you find women as distinguished, and minds as well cultivated, as in the capital. There are classes, I allow, but there are no distances. The gentleman is the same from one end of Great Britain to another.

The anxiety of the latter, when in the country, is to create himself a moral independence: instead of going to London, he attracts London to his house. To do this he receives new books, the reviews and papers. He is glad to have at his table travellers whom he knows, or who are recommended to him.

The arrangement of his house indicates a character of neatness and simplicity in wealth. At eight or nine in the morning the whole household is up. The family meet in the breakfast room when the daughters give mother and father the morning kiss – in the English fashion on one cheek – and where the stranger receives the serious and affectionate greetings of the family. A door opens, and all the servants, some seven or eight in number, enter one after the other, and in silence. When all are assembled, prayers are read, or else, in some sects, a chapter of the Bible is read! These religious customs may astonish a stranger, but in England where the difference in ranks is so marked, there is something touching in this admission of servants to the bosom of the family, that all may perform in common what is regarded as duty to the Deity. When prayers are over the family collect round the table, and drink tea or coffee. After breakfast while the master is generally engaged with his studies or business, the visitor has to occupy him agreeably – a large library, scientific collections, green-houses embellished with rare plants, and the gardens surrounding the house. At one o'clock there is lunch, or what is called in France the second breakfast. In the afternoon the family drive out to pay visits, explore the neighbourhood, or keep up with the farm and cottages those kindly relations which, to a certain point, fill up the difference in condition of persons in English society.

At six o'clock comes dinner: the ladies have changed their dress, and the gentlemen are in evening costume. The conversation is less animated and sparkling than in France, generally turning on serious subjects. One of the peculiarities of an English dinner is that after the dessert the ladies rise and leave the dining room, while the gentlemen seat themselves again and drink a few glasses of port. There is no hob-nobbing, but the master of the house who wishes to do honour to his guest, invites him to fill the glass: he does the same himself, and the couple exchange a bow before drinking.

About half an hour later all the company assemble in the drawing room which the servants enter in procession at about eleven o'clock. Evening prayers are then read, after which everyone retires to his bedroom after a friendly shake of the hand from all the members of the family.

In contrast, now, let us have a look into a labourer's cottage. A single ground-floor room serves at once as a kitchen, dining and drawing room. A wide open chimney, without grate, proves it was not intended to burn coal. The fuel formerly in use was roots, prickly furze and dried turf which, when raised in slabs, formed a species of peat. A wooden or stone bench placed in the interior of the chimney serves as family seat in the cold winter evenings.

The labourers frequently obtain from the farmer their supply of gorse and dried turf on condition they keep the ashes for him [as fertiliser]. A deal table, without a cloth, but carefully scrubbed, receives the coarse and substantial dishes which have been cooked in front of the fire on a hot iron plate. The family sits around the table on massive benches, generally fixed to the wall. If, by chance, there is an old chair in the house it is reserved for the grandmother. The children are more or less well tended according to the character of the place. In some cottages, little girls, bare-footed, with hair floating in disorder down their backs, and yet the stranger will be struck by their beauty, even when dressed in rags. Their large dark eyes, their complexion, rather brightened than burnt, by the sun, and their robust and well-developed limbs, evidently denote a great race.

Though the toilette of these persons may be more or less neglected, the room is generally very clean; the floor, washed every morning, is often sprinkled with fine sand through which the whiteness of the boards is plainly visible.

As soon as they have acquired the necessary strength, the wives and daughters attend out of doors in the stalls and fields to all sorts of rustic tasks, hence it is not unusual to find during daytime these cottages only guarded by a housekeeper of twelve years old. And that is not all, for the door remains open from morn till night to all comers with the simple confidence of persons who have nothing to defend.

The labourers regularly employed by a farmer generally get their wheat at a special price, fixed beforehand, for a whole year; those on the other hand who are not in regular employment arrange with the farmer for a piece of land, which they cultivate, in which case they pay rent or surrender part of the crop. With the remainder of the crop, the labourer manages to feed a pig, pay the rent of his cottage, and even rear some poultry. The family, more or less dispersed during the week, only comes together on

Saturday nights and Sunday. The peasants, as a rule, speak little and it is rather difficult to find a reason for this silence which at times resembles coldness.

In the towns, several learned societies have, during later years, greatly aided in developing agriculture as well as to increase the knowledge and improve the morals of the population. One of these Societies was the Polytechnic, founded by the Misses Fox in 1833. There is nothing particularly feminine about this. The meetings in Falmouth discuss science, political economy and industry. Falmouth was a good choice to serve as the place for these lectures and annual exhibitions. Meetings are well attended and several discoveries and useful improvements bring benefit to the members.

*

This is the first time a book has paid special attention to the blue bays of Cornwall, and I hope you, my patient reader now share with me regard and respect for the varied ingredients that make up their personalities. Certainly I hope that henceforth the sight of a bay on this ragged coast will be enriched for you by the facts I have been able to lay before you.

And so, I bid you farewell, and with warm thanks for your companionship.

N.T.

Appendixes, Bibliography and Index

Appendix A

What was a Privateer?

In the issue of the *Royal Cornwall Gazette* of 7 March 1801, it was reported that 'French privateers have recently been in the practice of insulting the coasts of Mount's Bay in the most audacious manner, frequently taking our coastal vessels within sight of the shores. To check these depredations in future, Government has ordered the *Valiant*, a fast sailing lugger of 14 guns, to be stationed in Mount's Bay; and, we trust, Lieut. Maxwell, who commands her, will soon give a good account of some of them.' What exactly was a privateer?

Whereas a pirate or a corsair was in the same category as a thief, a privateer was a vessel licensed by a Government to be armed (at the owner's expense) to capture any merchantman, or her cargo, whom she might be able to engage.

Provided the privateer carried on board her Commission, or licence, she would be accepted by her victim as an enemy naval vessel who would be entitled to seize her and her cargo as prize if the victim had been overpowered.

If, after an engagement, the captain of the privateer was unable to show his victim his licence, or *marque*, he was not complying with international law, and his Government would claim 'damages', and also the crew imprisoned were they to fall into enemy hands. It was, in fact, legalised robbery, adding to the complement of an established navy at minimum expense. One of the first, fabulously successful privateers was Sir Francis Drake.

It was by the Declaration of Paris, as late as 1856, that privateering was made illegal.

Appendix B

The Lanisley Letters

Turning to a copy of the *Journal of the Royal Institution of Cornwall* Vol VI Pt xxii page 374, we find extracts from a series of letters written by the steward of the Manor of Lanisley in Gulval, near Penzance, to his absentee-principals, the family of Onslow, in the course of the eighteenth century.

The letters tell no connected story but are rather 'Notes on the Times', made by men who knew the facts of the matters about which they wrote, and who had no more motive for doing other than recording them correctly. These extracts include perfectly trustworthy evidence of what a privateer might have done, for example, in Mount's Bay left defenceless in 1756. But the principal interest in the Letters concentrates around the account they give of smuggling and wrecking in Mount's Bay, in the middle of the eighteenth century:

From George Borlaise to Lieut. Gen. Onslow, 1st Feb., 1753
The late storms have brought several vessels ashore, and some dead wrecks. In the former case great barbarity has been committed, which a few soldiers would have prevented. And considering the coasts here swarm with smugglers from the Land's End to the Lizard by which an immense sum goes yearly to France, I wonder why they [the soldiers] without being replaced by others as they are, in these cases, of great use ...

From George Borlaise to Lieut. Gen. Onslow, 15 March, 1753
... I have often been an eye-witness of the barbarities at wrecks, and saved some ships myself with other help ... As to the soldiers I am sorry smuggling and wrecking are increased in these parts to such a degree as to render them necessary. The

riches of the land and sea are in full gallop to France, and the countenances given to the smugglers by those whose business it is to restrain those pernicious practices have brought them so bold and daring that no-one can venture to come near them with safety while they are at work. As to the wreck Bill I apprehend the adding of some preventive clause would make it an effective remedy against the habit of wrecking. My situation in life hath obliged me to sometimes be a spectator of things in it which shock humanity and which the Legislature intend some punishments for, but some things, I fear, this Bill will not reach.

The people who make it their business to attend these wrecks are generally Tynners, and as soon as they observe a ship on the coast, they first arm themselves with sharp axes and hatchets, and leave their mine to follow those ships. Sometimes the ship is not wrecked, but whether it is, or not, the mines suffer greatly not only for the loss of their labour which may be £100 a day if their number is 2,000 in quest of the ship, but where the water is quick the mine is drowned, and they seldom go *in a less number than 2,000* [my italics].

Now, it is hard to imagine how far the snatching of this infamous practice in its very bud. and laying the loss of all wages due, and some further penalty on every labouring miner who should leave his Tynwork in order to go to wreck, would contribute to keep them at home and break the neck of it.

The forfeitures would be certain loss, but the gain uncertain by going, supposing no punishment attended their plundering etc.

Next, I apprehend no person should be allowed to attend a wreck armed with axes or the like unless lawfully required. They'll cut a large trading vessel to pieces in one tide, and cut down everybody who offers to oppose them. Therefore, there should be some provision against this.

Next, I humbly apprehend the Bill does not sufficiently provide against the monstrous barbarity practised by those savages upon the poor sufferers. I have seen many a poor man, half dead, cast ashore and crawling out of the reach of the waves, fallen upon and in a manner stripp'd naked by those villains, and if, after, he has saved his chest or any more clothes, they have been taken from him. Inhuman and barbarous as this is, and although a Highwayman is a Christian compared to such, I think whoever should *forcibly* take any goods out of the possession of such ship-wrecked sailor by force, should suffer as Highwayman. [i.e. be hung].

George Borlaise to Lieut. Gen. Onslow, 15 Dec., 1750
I am sorry to tell you that, notwithstanding the late Act, there is as much occasion for soldiers as ever. Last Wednesday night a Dutchman was stranded near Helstone, every man saved and the ship whole, burthen 250 tons laden with claret. In 24 hours time the Tynners had cleared all, and a few months before they murdered a poor man just by Helstone who came in aid of a Custom House Officer to seize some brandy.

Bibliography

Cornwall and Scilly. Hencken, Methuen, London, 1932.

Excursions in Cornwall. Stockdale, Simpkin Marshall, London, 1824.

Itinerary of Cornwall. Cyrus Redding, Howard Parsons, London, 1842.

A Week at the Lizard. Rev. C.A. Johns, London, 1848.

Rambles Beyond Railways. Wilkie Collins, Bentley, London, 1851.

Rambles in Western Cornwall. J.O. Halliwell, Russell, London, 1861.

A Tour Through Cornwall. Rev. Richard Warner, Cruttwell, London, 1809.

Highways and Byways. Norway, Clay, London, 1897.

Carew's Survey of Cornwall, 1811

Parochial History of Cornwall, Davies Gilbert, Nicholls, vols. I, II, III, IV, London, 1838.

Cornwall and its Coasts. Alphonse Esquiros, Chapman & Hall, London, 1865.

The Land's End District. Edmonds, Russell Smith, London, 1862.

Lanisley Letters, RIC Journal, vol. VI Pt XXII.

Padstow's Lifeboats, Claude Berry, Lodenek Press, 1976.

Old Falmouth, Susan Gay, Headley Brothers, London, 1903.

The Merchant Schooners, Basil Greenhill, David and Charles, vols. I and II, Newton Abbot, 1951.

Cornwall and the Age of the Industrial Revolution. John Rowe, Liverpool University, 1953.

Smuggling in Cornwall. Cyril Noall, Bradford Barton, Cornwall, 1971.

Murder and Cannibalism. The Cornish Echo, June 29, 1923.

Life of Admiral Viscount Exmouth, Edward Osler, Smith Elder, London, 1835.

History of Cornwall. Richard Polwhele, Cadell and Davis, London, 1803.

The Harveys of Hayle. Edmund Vale, D. Bradford Barton, Truro, 1966.

The Cornish Coast. Charles Harper, Chapman and Hall, London, 1910.

The Autobiography of a Smuggler. ed. by John B. Cornish, Truro, 1894.

The Wreck of the Saint Anthony. John Chynoweth, RIC Journal, New Series, vol. V part IV 1968, p.385.

Memories and Opinions by 'Q' (Sir Arthur Quiller-Couch), ed. by S.C. Roberts, Cambridge University Press, 1944.

Index